HOW F*** DID I GET HERE?

CHLOE KENT

Copyright © Chloe Kent 2025

All rights reserved. The right of Chloe Kent to be identified as the author of this work has been asserted in accordance with the Copyright, Designs, and Patents Act 1988.

No part of this publication may be altered, reproduced, distributed, or transmitted in any form, by any means, including, but not limited to, scanning, duplicating, uploading, hosting, distributing, or reselling, without the express prior written permission of the publisher, except in the case of reasonable quotations in features such as reviews, interviews, and certain other non-commercial uses currently permitted by copyright law.

PROLOGUE

Blue chairs, white walls and a few leaflets about fun days out littered on the basic round coffee table. It is the least appealing room in this place which is a shame because the rest of the building feels like a four-star hotel. Well, the type of four-star hotel that confiscates shoelaces, belts and electronics upon check-in. But still, it's a decent place and I know that compared to many other mental health facilities, I am really fortunate to have landed myself in this one.

Today, I have visitors, which is why I find myself in the unappealing visitors' lounge. I'm really not a fan of it. It's the one room that looks and feels very clinical which makes it awkward when college friends drop by. I don't know why it bothers me – it's obvious where I am, but it just feels extra obvious in this room.

My friends don't tend to ask me why I'm here or to fish for any of the gritty details. If anything, they just drop in like they did when they would come over to my house – they chat about unserious topics and spend most of the duration ripping the piss out of each other, just like they did at college. The benefits of having male friends are exactly this. There's no digging for information, no gossip, no prying; they turn up with great banter, make me laugh and promise to come back another day. It's really that easy. And looking back, really quite heartwarming.

We were just seventeen-year-old kids in college; they had no clue about why I was an inpatient in a secure mental health hospital. I have no doubt that visiting me must have been fairly daunting. It's an impressive but old building that looks quite intimidating from the outside and, once you get inside, the doors automatically lock behind you and only a staff member can let you out again. You have to give your name at the desk and wait a moment whilst they check if the patient is allowed visitors, which they usually are unless they've tried to hurt themselves or run away. I'm sitting here at thirty-five years old feeling quite moved that two teenagers did that for me. We lost touch along the way; it happens in life doesn't it? But I hope they know how grateful I am for their visits.

But one particular day, the visit isn't quite as uneventful as previous ones. As the lads get ready to head out, we barely make it through our goodbyes before a horrendously loud, shrill alarm rips through the air causing all the staff around us to rush to the office to check whose room has the emergency.

I hate this sound; I luckily haven't heard it too often but it's an unforgiving deafening sound that makes me feel instantly sick. It's the most urgent alarm in this place which means somebody is in serious need of help. Each room is fitted with an emergency red cord which must only be pulled in the most urgent times. Sometimes a patient pulls it themselves, occasionally they've hurt themselves or want to end their life but change their mind at the last minute and pull the string; sometimes a staff member will pull it if they've gone to check on a patient and they aren't responding.

That happened last week. A young patient, only sixteen, managed to somehow grab a bunch of tablets from the medicine cupboard when the head nurse had his back turned; she went back to her room and swallowed every single one. She spent the next three nights in Tunbridge Wells hospital and when she came back, she was yellow for a week. It was a stark reminder of why we are all here. Because on the surface, she was just another teenage girl who likes to have a laugh and a chat and to watch movies – but given half a chance, she'll end her life. Not because she wants to die. But because she wants to end the pain. That's the difference I have come to understand in life.

I remember watching through the glass to the staffroom as one of the nurses checks the board to see which room has the alarm going off.

"ROOM ELEVEN!" she screams as half a dozen staff members rush towards it, including one of the head doctors; he is usually upstairs on the adult ward, but he appears at the double doors, frantic and desperate to quickly get to whoever needs his help.

I am so taken aback by all the commotion that it doesn't even register which patient belongs to room eleven at first. But then I realise: it's me. That emergency alarm is coming from my room.

CHAPTER ONE
HOW IT STARTED

Although I've titled this chapter *How it started,* the truth is that pinpointing exactly when it started is incredibly difficult. I don't feel as if there was a day when I just woke up like this. A part of me believes I just came out of the womb this way. There's that saying isn't there – *born worrier* – and I think that's me. I think to some degree I was always an anxious kid but as I got older it became harder to control until eventually it affected my whole life. So, although I can't pinpoint the start, I can pinpoint when it worsened and that was in the year 2003 when I was fourteen years old, after my dad finally decided after years of being in a loveless marriage that it was time to get a divorce. My mum took it as well as Will Smith takes a joke about his wife. And that is when the problems begun.

When my dad told me he was leaving, I knew I had to go too. There were so many reasons why I came to this decision, but the main one was that living with Mum alone, without my dad, simply terrified me. My mum could be a whole array of things that I imagined would only be a lot worse without my dad around. She was often neglectful, in the sense that I barely spoke to her; she'd sit in her bedroom most of the time, usually watching hours of television, the *EastEnders* omnibus mostly. How many times can a woman watch Den and Angie Watts come to blows on Christmas day? A lot apparently. And that trumped most things for her – like talking to her kids or making them a proper dinner. She wasn't purposely neglecting me; she was just who she was.

Dad took the last of our bags and placed them in the boot of the car. "Go and say goodbye to your mum," he said so quietly, probably hoping I wouldn't hear the emotion in his voice, but I heard it. "Tell her you'll be back to see her at the weekend." I noticed a single tear fall down his cheek. I didn't expect him to cry, he never cries. I realise now though that saying goodbye to twenty years of marriage still hurts, even when you can't stand the person.

I reluctantly walked back through the front door and into the house. The music was blaring so loudly – Mum had Whitney Houston's "I will always love you" blasting from the television on volume one hundred. Cringe. That sounds harsh but I remember feeling that. I felt so awkward walking into the living room to find her in her usual place, in front of the TV. She was crying, the sort of crying where it's so hard that you barely make a sound. I hated that moment; I still hate it when I think about it. She looked so weak and so helpless. I wasn't used to seeing her that way. She was Carol Harding after all. No fucks given, quick wit, dry humour, Carol who would tell you how it is and not care who she upset in the process. And yet here she was, looking so much smaller than I'd ever seen her and grieving for a marriage that was over long before today.

"Dad said he'll bring me back over at the weekend Mum," I mumbled. She barely acknowledged the words, so I tried again to reassure her. "It's only a few days away, I'll see you really soon." I realised something in that moment: Mum wasn't worried about seeing me again at the weekend. She just wanted her loveless marriage back because existing with Dad was easier for her than existing without him.

I left her crying on the sofa in the foetal position and assured Dad that I had promised her I'd be back to see her. What I didn't tell him, however, was that I didn't think she cared either way. I felt like I lost my mum that day, at least the version of her I'd known, and it would be ten years until I had her back again.

***

It was three forty-five in the morning when my mum called my phone for the umpteenth time. I didn't want to answer but I had to. The last three voicemails she had left were her threatening to kill herself if I didn't answer and I was getting scared that if I didn't do as I was told, she'd carry out those threats.

Is that what you want for your mum, Chloe? To die?

I'll do it and it will be your fault. Everyone will know it was your fault because you didn't care about your own mum.

That was the gist of the voice messages and phone calls that I had been receiving most nights for the best part of a year. Mum had developed a dangerous drinking habit – she'd wake up late in the day, around three or four in the afternoon, start drinking by five and then, as the early hours rolled around and she was a bottle of vodka in, the phone calls would start. It always began with abuse, then the threats, then often she'd phone back just to sing me a bit of ABBA. I quite like that she mixed it up to be honest. "Fernando" was my favourite. She didn't know enough of the words to "Waterloo" so that tended to be painful.

One particular night, however, I had my best friend from school sleeping over at my house when Mum called with this incredible *Thelma and Louise* style idea. I was to sneakily pack a bag, grab my passport, leave the house without Dad knowing, go and meet Mum somewhere at almost four o'clock in the morning and run away to France with her, never to be seen again. However, she had overlooked two things. Number one: running away with a binge-drinking narcissist having a manic episode was about as appealing as being babysat by Myra Hindley. And number two: I was with my best friend.

"She can come too!" Mum suggested when I pointed out this small matter.

I looked at Amy and fear momentarily flashed in her eyes. For a second, she wondered whether I'd accept this crazy offer and try and persuade her to go on this road trip with crazy Carol, waking up in Calais tomorrow with new names like Genevieve or Thierry Henry. As much as I do love a middle of the night road trip, I think this would be taking the piss.

I calmly explained to my own mum that I couldn't run away with her because I had plans to finish my GCSEs and stay in England. But perhaps another time. Of course, this didn't sit well with my mum who had probably had her heart set on this plan for the whole ten minutes before she called me. So, she took an overdose of painkillers and antidepressants and left multiple voice messages informing me that this was what I had done to her. The final voice message was her saying that she could see the light before she finally called her own ambulance and thankfully made a full recovery.

She went on to repeat this pattern until I was so consumed by fear, guilt and worry that I stopped being able to sleep at night. I remember dreading the phone calls starting so much that I could never settle. I'd go to school on barely any sleep and didn't realise how unwell it was making me until things got even worse. Mum had become angry. She was no longer threatening to hurt herself, but she was threatening to hurt my dad. My mum knew dodgy people from back in the day, people who, if offered money, might come for my dad. They might hurt him.

One day, when I was visiting my mum on a weekend, I saw a name scribbled on a piece of paper and would later learn that she'd done it. She had contacted somebody to hurt Dad. I didn't know when or where, but I told Dad what I had seen. For months, I lived in fear. I remember one evening, somebody knocked on our front door; my dad jumped off the sofa and grabbed the closest thing he could use as a weapon which happened to be a fire poker. He shouted through the door and demanded to know who it was. The person didn't answer. I swear to God, if someone had said "Is Tamara home?", like in that Liv Tyler movie *The Strangers*, I'd have passed away right there and then.

My mum had successfully terrified me in my own home. Thankfully, there wasn't a dangerous man on the other side of the door, but unfortunately, it was my mum. She'd found out our new address and thought she'd rock up for a visit. We didn't answer the door and she eventually left.

I wonder about my dad's fear now, how he felt about the possibility somebody might come into our home and hurt him in front of me. Like most good parents, he probably didn't even care for himself, but rather what that scene would do to me. How traumatised it could have left me.

Now that Mum had our address, nothing was stopping her. She would drive to our house in the middle of the night and slash the tyres on the car, then the next day she'd come back and throw a plant pot through the windscreen. I remember one morning, Dad had to drive me to school in the damaged car; he had one hand on the steering wheel and one hand trying to shield me from any of the broken glass that could fly into my face.

That was my mum. She wanted to hurt my dad so much that she didn't care if she was hurting me too and, my god, she really was. My sleep was so poor now because every sound kept me on a knife edge. I worried about what could happen next.

I used to creep into my dad's bedroom at night and look out of his window, keeping an eye on the driveway just in case somebody approached the house. In my head, I thought that as long as I was keeping a lookout, I could phone the police before anyone could make it inside and maybe they'd arrive before anyone could hurt us. But I'd need to stay alert, I couldn't risk being in a deep sleep because then I wouldn't hear anyone coming.

In the end, nobody ever came, but I had developed this anxiety about nighttime and going to bed. The second I got into bed and settled, I'd start with this horrible breathless feeling, it was like each breath was restricted and wasn't going all the way back into my lungs. With each breath feeling more unsatisfying than the last, I'd end up in a panic, my heart would get faster, I'd feel restless, scared, fearful, I'd cry and no matter what, I couldn't relax.

Eventually, I had to tell Dad, I was too scared not to. I kept feeling like I was going to die, it felt like something was physically wrong with me. I remember Dad telling me he used to have these feelings a lot as a teenager too and he called them the *what ifs*. What if I don't do well in my GCSEs? What if I can't get tickets for Busted? What if I forget my PE kit? I got the idea – and it made a lot of sense. Except mine were more like:

What if my mum kills herself? What if something bad happens to my dad? What if Mum hurts us?

The next year remained eventful where my mum was concerned. She sent funeral brochures to the house, death threats and more. But my personal favourite was when I rocked up to school one day to find out from my head of year that Mum had phoned the school that morning and told them I had died. DIED. And she didn't even have the good grace to produce a story as to how I died. Which really bugged me for the rest of the day. If I'm deceased in my mum's warped brain, then I'd like to know what happened! My best friend and I decided I was hit by one of those air balloons in the end. It sounded good. All jokes aside, my head of year's face was a picture when I walked in. I bet that was a fun story for the staffroom that day.

That was the final straw for my dad. Whilst going through the courts to get their divorce granted, he also managed to get some kind of protection order in place. For the next few months, my mum couldn't call my phone or harass my life. It was all fun and games when the order was lifted, but for a while, it was a nice breather in between.

CHAPTER TWO
THREE YEARS LATER

It's nighttime, almost midnight actually, and Dad has me in the car driving to a twenty-four-hour Tesco. He suggested we buy some Airwaves or extra strong mints; something that may help me feel like I am breathing. In theory, it's not a bad idea. On the way back home, I lay back against the headrest, chewing enough Airwaves that I swear it's burning my brain, but it's not necessarily making me feel like I can breathe any better.

"Why am I suffering like this, Dad?" I cry. Hot tears escape my eyes. I'm too tired to hold it together. It's so exhausting feeling this way. All. The. Time. I don't feel like a seventeen-year-old girl at all. I feel like a little child who keeps falling over and scraping her knees and needs her dad to pick her up again. And again. This must be exhausting for him too.

"I don't know baby; we'll get you home and I'll make you a cup of tea." One cup of tea and two episodes of *Friends* later and I finally feel my body relaxing enough to be able to go to bed.

"See, you just needed a good old cup of tea," Dad jokes as I thank him for the hundredth time for sitting up with me and head upstairs for sleep.

***

A lot can change in three years. My dad met somebody new, and they got married; he bought a new house with his new wife, and we all lived together somewhere where my mum definitely didn't know. And to be honest, I had been feeling a lot happier; my interactions with Mum had been minimal because she still wasn't herself. She'd still take any opportunity to hurt me, just so that in turn, it hurt my dad. I did think a while back that she was getting better, she was really chirpy on the phone; turns out she had invited two Australian backpackers to live with her for a few weeks and they'd introduced her to a bong. So she wasn't better. She was just high. She sang me A LOT of ABBA in those few weeks the Aussie lads were there.

I couldn't work out why though, if I had been happier, if I'd been sleeping fine, going to school fine and socialising without problems, why I now felt back to square one. Why was I struggling to sleep? Why did nighttime scare me so much? Why couldn't I see anyone or do anything without getting anxious? Why had I developed agoraphobia? I know now that this was just a very typical example of PTSD, mixed with the prolonged stress of putting up with my mum. I had cut her out plenty of times to try and protect myself, but I always felt guilty and would go back. I just felt like she was really on her own otherwise – she didn't really have many friends anymore and my older sister had her own life. I never wanted her to be alone, I just wanted her to be better so I could cope with being around her.

Whilst most of my friends were now clubbing, since they were either already eighteen or seventeen with fake IDs, I spent my evenings at home binge-watching *Will & Grace*. I'd become such a recluse that people stopped inviting me out, they just knew I wasn't going to leave the house. I'd go to college during the day and come home, that was it. But even college was proving too difficult. I realised I was clock watching, counting down the minutes for the class to end so that I could go back outside and breathe. Sitting in a classroom was really tough, I felt trapped and anxious; knowing I couldn't just get up and leave made my anxiety a hundred times worse.

It wasn't long before I was walking home halfway through the day because I couldn't complete any of my lessons. Being out of the house was terrifying, but frustratingly, I didn't feel much safer at home, it was just that I could be anxious in private at home. Nobody could see me freaking out. I was hidden away.

The next few months in the run-up to me being taken to the mental health unit are a bit of a blur. My dad was trying everything to help me get better. He took me to a top-of-the-range psychotherapist in Cambridge and we would drive there every week for two-hour sessions. He'd wait outside. My stepmum found some herbal tablets online that were raved about for anxiety and my dad bought them for me. I'll never forget the smell – it was like yeast and fart.

The next part I'm about to write, only a very few people know about. I particularly hid it from my dad, so Dad, if somehow you're reading this, please skip ahead.

I'll tell it in brief because the person in question isn't worth the ink on the page. I met a boy at college. I quickly became his girlfriend, and he very quickly became controlling and abusive. I didn't realise how often he was doing it until it was too late. One day at college, he asked me to spend the night at his house. I said I couldn't because my anxiety had been bad. He produced a video on his phone which was of me doing something sexual for him. He threatened to send it to my dad. From that moment on, he knew he had me in the palm of his hand and he threatened me with it at every chance he could to get his own way. He began texting me late at night, telling me to sneak out of my house and meet him somewhere. I had to tread very carefully. I couldn't risk making him mad. I'd produce what I thought were decent excuses as to why I couldn't meet him but none of them were good enough. He'd text me with threats of sending the video, telling me how disappointed and disgusted my dad would be with me. He'd tell me how he'd never look at me the same way ever again and our close relationship would be ruined forever.

It felt like I was thrown back to 2003 again. I was

scared at nighttime. Scared of what could happen. Scared to sleep, just in case. My dad used to leave his mobile phone in the kitchen at night and I would creep downstairs regularly to check he hadn't been sent the video. I wasn't getting to sleep until five o'clock most mornings and when I was awake, I lived in fear, convinced that at any moment somebody was going to drop this bomb on my life and I'd lose my relationship with my dad, the one person who had looked after me unconditionally.

Now, as a thirty-five-year-old with my own children, I realise that even if he had sent that video, my dad would still have loved me unconditionally. Of course, it's not a video any father wants to see of their daughter, but I was seventeen years old, I wasn't doing anything everyone else in relationships my age was doing. My dad was certainly doing the same at my age. It was normal. But what wasn't normal was being coerced and controlled by someone who had filmed me against my will. He'd have been the one who would have ended up in a mountain of trouble, not me. But I was too naïve at seventeen to realise this.

I must have felt trapped with no way out. Because the next thing I knew I'd become obsessed with the idea of ending my life and that final straw led to me packing my bags ready to be admitted to the young person's mental health unit.

CHAPTER THREE

IT'S GIVING 'GIRL INTERRUPTED'.

I thought top dogs were only supposed to be in prisons, turns out they're in mental health hospitals too. If I'd watched *Girl Interrupted* by this time, I'd have known that I had just came face to face with Lisa Rowe played by Angelina Jolie. Although that probably is a bit unfair to the girl, she didn't seem like trouble, but she certainly seemed like a piece of the furniture here.

It's a strange first day in a ward like this one. I get introduced to my bedroom, almost like I'm a visitor at a fancy hotel being shown around by a porter. The staff try to make me as relaxed and as comfortable as possible and then they search my bag and take half my stuff. For safety reasons of course, but still, so many rules. No shoelaces, no belts, no hair bands, nothing I can strangle myself with. Then no mouthwash, no face cleansers, nothing with alcohol in it that I could potentially drink.

I laughed at first and wondered if I looked like the sort of person who was lining up shots of Oral-B in the evening. Turns out, though, a fair few of the inpatients absolutely would drink my mouthwash given half the chance. Fair enough. I also lost any right to my phone – it's a distraction and allows people from the outside world to possibly affect your recovery. I didn't realise it to begin with but living without any access to my phone was about to be the best rule I could follow. A certain college boy couldn't contact me, and he certainly couldn't threaten me with any videos.

I remember looking around my room, which had a little en-suite, and thinking how suicide-proof everything was. I was even informed that I'd need to ask for a plug when I wanted to take a bath to ensure I didn't attempt to drown myself at any other time. Then I was informed that for the first week somebody would sit with me whilst I bathed and would watch me the entire time. I briefly had hope that it might be a six-foot tattooed man with a beard, however, unfortunately for me, it was a fifty-year-old Jamaican lady called Gloria. Gloria was ok, but I'd soon learn that she was extremely strict; most days, she only let me fill the bathtub a quarter of the way to be extra safe. As a plus-size girl, that meant the water was barely above my minge; anyway, I managed.

Later that first day, I met more of the patients. I was far too scared to leave my room so most of them came by my door and hovered there until I noticed them and introduced themselves. The first girl who approached me had the biggest grin; she seemed much younger than me, maybe thirteen, and she looked so happy, like this was the best ever place to be. "Welcome to the madhouse!" she said, like it was a good thing. I forced a smile, gave her a nod, and thanked her. Thanked her for what exactly, I'm not sure. But maybe compared to where she came from, this was the best place. I don't exactly know her history.

Next up was Jimbo. He turned up at my door wearing three t-shirts, two hoodies and two pairs of jeans. He was probably nearing six feet; he looked younger than me, probably sixteen, although the way he spoke you'd think he was only around eight years old. He spoke with such excitement and enthusiasm you couldn't help but find him endearing. He told me how happy he was to be seeing a new fresh face and how I kind I looked. He said if I needed anything, I should just ask him. Then, before he abruptly walked off, he said if I touched his Pokémon collection he'd tell on me.

Before I knew it, the top dog was back. I'll refer to her as Lisa since we've referenced the movie already. She hung around my door, not really saying much, almost as if she was sizing me up. When she smiled, I noticed some missing teeth and when she put her arms against my door frame I saw hundreds of healed scars, although some looked only recently healed. I had a few of my own self-harming scars, but nothing like hers. You'd be lucky to find unmarked skin on her arms, it was the worst I'd ever seen.

"You'll get your diagnosis probably by Monday when you see Maddie, the therapist."

"Oh." I nodded, I didn't actually know that. So far, I had seen one male therapist who was the head of our department; he was the one who told my dad to bring me here, he was the one who would make all the decisions on my life for next few weeks or so.

I hadn't even thought about any other possible diagnosis really. Ever since I was fifteen, my GP just told me it was a generalised anxiety disorder and depression. Both really common and both easily treated. If only he could see me right now – boy, was he wrong.

I look up, realising that Lisa is still in my doorway, arms propped above her head, bags of confidence. She's staring at me to the point where it's quickly becoming uncomfortable.

"Well, thanks for letting me know," I say.

"When you get your diagnosis, make sure you come and find me. I want to know what you're in here for." I think about asking why but before I can even speak, she disappears again. I realise I probably know why – if she's some kind of top dog in this place, then I suppose she feels it's her duty to know everything about everyone. Me included. She appears to be around my age, seventeen going on eighteen, but she behaves much older.

I spend the next hour or so in my room, unpacking and taking in my surroundings. Not that there's much to take in. I have a window with a view of a field and a single bed with a bedside table; for now I have propped my portable CD player on it. There is also a desk and chair, for writing down my mental thoughts I presume, and a huge whiteboard on my wall, for what exactly, I don't know. My bedroom door has a window that cannot be covered at any time so that the nurses can check-in as they wish. For now, I am on half-hour checks, which basically means every thirty minutes somebody shines a torch into my room and makes sure I'm not bouncing off the walls or digging a hole like the *Great Escape*. Luckily for them, I am doing neither of those things. I am actually listening to Sean Paul and trying to work out if it's culturally appropriate to ask Gloria to give me corn rows.

I'm two verses into trying to rap along to "Temperature" when a nurse I haven't seen before comes straight in without knocking.

"Chloe, I have on my paperwork that you get most anxious at night and you're not sleeping. I'll give you until ten o'clock tonight, if you're not asleep by then, Dr Paul said I'm to give you something to help you sleep."

Dr Pope is the one I said is now in charge of my life for the next few weeks. The head psychologist here. The idea of a sleeping tablet really doesn't sit well with me, I have never taken anything like that before, plus new things make me anxious – I once had a panic attack after a Gaviscon! I want to argue with her that I don't want to take anything like that but she's giving strong matron vibes and I don't think she'll let me have my own way.

I shrug and half-heartedly agree.

"Chloe, we need to get you understanding about sleep health, do you know what that is?"

I shake my head. Almost certain she just made it up.

She huffs a little like I'm being challenging.

"It means in order to have a good night's sleep you'll need to do the appropriate things to ensure that happens. For example, no music after nine o'clock so you can wind down, I advise a warm drink as well and, most importantly, you need the correct clothing for sleep. Thin pyjamas are best, loose fitting too. So many of you teenagers these days fall asleep in your hoodies and God knows what else, it is so unhealthy. Our bodies need to breathe as well."

This bitch is looking at me like I've been going to bed in a hazmat suit. I can feel the back of my neck prickling with heat, I'm getting wound up. I feel like she can't possibly understand a single thing about my anxiety if she is suggesting half the problem is that I'm not wearing the right pyjamas. It's almost insulting.

I make a point to pull out my pyjamas from the chest of drawers in the corner of the room and assure her I am doing the right things to give myself every chance of a good night's sleep. My clothing is fine. It's my brain that's not.

She nods and scribbles something down on her notes.

"And dinner? You didn't go down to eat with everybody else earlier, why is that?"

"I just wasn't hungry yet," I lie. I was hungry, but the thought was so daunting. Breakfast and dinner are served in the main dining room which is out of our unit and across the hall; it is also where the adult patients from upstairs go for food. I am absolutely not brave enough yet to eat in a room with that many people, especially people with so many different mental illnesses. What if someone here is really crazy and tries to stab me with their fork? What if one can't control what they say and shouts "run big bitch" or something when I walk into the room? It'll be like sports day all over again. Not for me.

"That's fine for tonight," she answers without lifting her eyes up from the clipboard on which she's been scribbling. "But for good sleep, you should eat something – there's cheese, rolls, crackers and hot drinks in the kitchen next door, go and help yourself. Everyone else is still down in the dining room so you'll have the room to yourself."

Well, not quite to myself since the nurses will be around, but the thought of not being with all the other patients yet is appealing. Once Miss Sleep Health has gone, I get changed into my pyjamas, throw on some slippers and walk to the kitchen. It's not quite next door to me, there are two more rooms in between. I'm actually impressed when I get to the kitchen – it's huge and open plan with a spacious living area, a few sofas, a large television with some plastic screen over it and further on it opens up to a big conservatory that looks inviting. I had no idea it was going to be quite this big. The cupboards are well stocked too with teabags, decaf coffee and hot chocolates. Just as sleep health woman said, there's a whole tray of mini white rolls, cheeses, spreads and biscuits. I make myself a hot chocolate and get stuck into some of the rolls.

I get comfy at the table but I'm only a few bites into my roll when I hear the commotion of people arriving back. I hear the door bleep as it opens, a tonne of footsteps and voices as people chat back and forth in conversation. I want to try and run back to my room, but the kitchen is so close to the entrance they'll all see me, and I don't want to purposely look like I'm avoiding them. I don't want them to think I'm rude.

I decide to try and front it out, act nonchalant and unphased. I'm fine. I'm just new, so it's a bit daunting, but really there is nothing to be scared about. All these people are just like me, just people who want to get better.

"Hi," a girl with blonde hair says with a smile. She is actually the first patient here to have a gentle tone to her voice and I instantly warm to her and decide she's the least threatening person in here. "I'm Katie."

"Chloe," I say with a smile back.

"What are you in here for?"

"She hasn't got her diagnosis yet; Maddie wasn't in today." Lisa barges in and answers for me. She pulls out a chair and sits opposite me, instantly swinging back on it like she's just chilling in some youth centre and not a hospital.

"Oh… I'm in here because I keep trying to kill myself. I hear voices telling me to do it and I have a severe panic disorder and a personality disorder," Katie explains. It amazes me how relaxed her tone is when she tells me. There is no shame or fear of being judged, she just opens up and it's kind of nice. I feel less alone.

"Hey Jim!" Lisa shouts out as Jimbo walks into the kitchen shuffling some of his Pokémon cards in his hands. "Why don't you tell Chloe what you're in here for?" I quickly notice the smirk as her lips curl up. Maybe it's an inside joke or maybe it's a really funny story.

"Oh yes Lisa! I'd love to!" he answers with all the enthusiasm of an excitable child on Christmas Eve.

Jimbo approaches the table; he looks even taller now I'm sat down.

"It was nighttime, and my parents said I had to go to bed, and I was really cross because I wasn't even tired. I didn't *want* to go to bed. But they didn't listen to me, and I got angrier and angrier, so then I had a plan. I went to bed but I stayed awake. I waited until my *parents* went to bed and then I waited a bit longer until I knew they were definitely asleep. And then I crept downstairs, out into the garden and into my dad's shed. I retrieved this hand axe he has that he says I'm not allowed to touch, and I went back inside with it, up the stairs, and…"

"Jim! That's enough," health sleep lady blurts out from the doorway. "I don't want you getting all worked up before bed, ok?"

"Ok, Miss Holland. Sorry."

I'm *sorry*. What the actual fuck? Was Jimbo about to tell me he murdered his parents with an AXE? A *fucking axe*? His bedroom is opposite mine! How the hell am I supposed to sleep now? My bed is twenty feet away from a psychotic axe-wielding murderer who wears three jumpers and is addicted to Pokémon. Jesus Christ. Lisa looks amused. She wanted me to be scared. Well, it has definitely worked. Miss Holland wanted me to be asleep by ten o'clock – well there's no fucking chance of that.

CHAPTER FOUR
DELULU IS THE SOLULU

I had my first sleeping pill that night. It was obvious after Jimbo's terrifying bedtime story that I wasn't going to settle with ease. I was sure I could fool Miss Holland into thinking I was asleep; I mean I used to do it all the time when I was kid. I hated going to bed straight after *Eastenders* so I once pretended that I'd fallen asleep on the sofa. It worked until my mum said, "What a shame Chloe is asleep. She's going to miss out on all this chocolate cake." Of course, I peeked to see if she was bullshitting me or whether there really was cake. I played right into her hands. My mum was stood over me, one hand on her hip, looking smug that she had tricked me. No chocolate cake in sight. Damn me and my obesity.

Miss Holland was harder to trick, and she ended up persuading me to take my first sleeping tablet. She said the first step to getting better was a better sleep routine, so I popped the tablet and within twenty minutes my eyelids were so heavy that I was falling asleep before eleven o'clock, which hadn't happened in a long, long time. Then she had the audacity to wake me up just before her shift ended at 6:55am by tickling my feet. Yes, tickling my feet. What kind of sick demonic place was I in?

"Come on Chloe. Jump in the shower and get dressed. A good sleep routine means you are up fresh and early."

Yes well, it's certainly early, but I don't feel fresh.

"With all due respect Miss Holland, I'm off my nut still on the sleeping tablets you gave me. I feel groggy, I need to go back to sleep."

"Nope!" She claps her hands together before whipping the blanket off me and opening the curtains. "You have to fight through it, you'll sleep so much better tonight, trust me."

I hate that saying: *You'll sleep well tonight!* I'd rather sleep now if it's all the same.

Miss Holland is like the weirdest drug dealer ever – she supplies the goods and then doesn't even let me ride the wave. The only good thing about taking the tablet was that I had hoped I could sleep the day away. But she's made it clear that she isn't leaving my room until I'm up and dressed. So, I give in, throw on a tracksuit and head to the kitchen for a drink. I am of course the first one up – no one else appears until around eight o'clock.

Katie is the first to appear which I'm happy about,

she's by far the most approachable. We chat over a cup of tea, and I learn that she lives around the corner from my sister and went to school with friends I had. Overall, she seems like the sort of person I could call a friend.

Next to appear is Lisa who looks me up and down and then bursts out laughing. "They gave you the sleeping tablets, didn't they?"

I didn't think it was *that* obvious. I do look slightly dishevelled I suppose, and my complexion is much paler than yesterday, but Jesus.

"You look out of it. It's alright though, you get used to them pretty quick."

I sip my tea but don't answer her, I don't exactly want to get *used* to it. Relying on tablets wasn't what I wanted for myself. It's not that I don't doubt they could help, but of course with my anxiety I'm already worrying about side effects and long-term use – what if I get addicted? I'll end up on Dr Phil.

As nine o'clock nears, I find myself following behind the rest of our unit as we head to the dining room for breakfast. I'll have to go down for proper food eventually, so it may as well be now. We meet some of the adults halfway there as a few patients start appearing on the stairs. Most look worse than us 'kids'. Not many seem very bright or refreshed this morning. I think about offering a polite smile, but I can't imagine any smiling back, so I keep myself to myself instead, walk past reception and head into the large dining room with a buffet filled with cereals, cooked breakfasts, croissants, fruit and yogurts. I'm ushered to one of the large round tables where two nurses sit with Katie, Lisa, Jimbo and another guy I haven't spoken to yet. His name is Tom and he looks to be my age; he has ginger hair and quite a scruffy appearance. I notice his jaw is always dropped open, like he is falling asleep or off his nut on muscle relaxants so much that he can't be bothered to close his mouth.

The breakfast starts fine, uneventful. Lisa gets a full English breakfast, Katie sticks with cereal and I'm too nervous to eat loads so I just pick at some plain toast. I'd kill for some Marmite but most of the adult patients are at the buffet now and I don't fancy getting in their way. I sit back and people watch, trying to work out why some of them are here and feeling sad that so many are.

One man approaches the table next to us with his plate of eggs and toast. He is probably mid-thirties, Asian; he catches my eye and briefly offers an empathic smile. His eyes are what I notice first – they're red and puffy like he has just been crying or is severely sleep deprived. I don't know why, but it's upsetting to see. I notice Tom start fidgeting in the corner of my eye, he's looking bored and scanning the room, for what I don't know. Suddenly his eyes still on the Asian man who smiled at me.

"What's Bin Laden doing here?" he asks so loudly that the majority of the room turn to look at our table. My jaw drops open. My eyes flit between Tom, who I now think is a massive bellend, and the innocent man sitting across from us pouring milk into his coffee.

"Shhh! Thomas! Or you'll go back to your room," says one of the nurses.

Tom is completely undeterred by that threat. "Oi, Bin Laden, don't go bombing me." Nobody is laughing or encouraging him in anyway, but he oddly smirks as if they are.

"Shut up Tom, you prick," Lisa pipes up as she attempts to grab Tom's t-shirt. He is standing now, waving his pointer finger in the direction of the Asian guy who looks as though he is doing his best to pay him no attention.

"Oi, I'm talking to you, terrorist wanker."

Tom looks like he is about to go over and physically attack the poor guy when a male nurse intervenes; both the nurses from our table also get up and help restrain him, ushering him away and presumably taking him back to the ward as quickly as possible. I look back at the poor guy whose day started by being racially attacked before he'd even had his breakfast. Sadly, he looks as though that outburst from Tom was the very least of his problems. I wish I could say something, but I'm seventeen – what is the right thing to do here? Do I speak up? Or will Tom attack me? I'm not sure I can cope with that.

I spend the next half an hour of my breakfast checking on the guy at the opposite table. He gives nothing away – I don't know if he is sad, angry, offended or just brushing it off as some mentally ill boy from the kid's ward. One thing I do know though is that I'm angry. As soon as I'm allowed, I'm leaving the table and gunning for Tom back at the ward.

As suspected, when we get back, Tom is slumped in

front of the television catching up with some football highlights. I barely know him, but it hasn't taken long to see that Tom is incredibly lazy. It's like it's an effort just to breathe for him. He does not look the slightest bit guilty either.

"Alright?" I ask, standing in the way of the TV to be extra annoying.

"Move out of the way, this is my team!"

"Nah. Why did you have to talk to that man like that? Where do you get off?"

He shrugs, his jaw slack as always. "I didn't want to eat breakfast with a terrorist."

"Obviously he's not a terrorist, you're just an idiot, you should be embarrassed. That was proper nasty."

"Oh well." He shrugs again. "I hate it here. I'll probably be discharged next weekend anyway, I got to get back to Portsmouth and sort my boys out, we got games to win."

Sort his boys out? What?

"What do you mean?"

He lifts his head proudly. "I own Portsmouth FC, that's my club, they're my boys. I'm a millionaire, I bought them last year."

I look him up and down, unconvinced. He has a cigarette burn hole in his jeans by the crotch and his blue shirt has week-old stains on it. His thick orange hair is overgrown and he has thick black dirt under each of his fingernails.

"Why are you here then?"

"I don't know. I was just walking to the shops one

day and I got bundled into the back of a van. It's all a mistake. I have to get back; my glamour model girlfriend is waiting for me at home in our million-pound apartment."

"Glamour model?"

"Yes, she used to do page three. She's begging for me to come home. That's why I don't talk to the girls in here much, they all want to sleep with me."

Ok, he is delulu. Maybe in his warped mind he genuinely thought he was in danger earlier, I don't know, but if he believes he is a millionaire football manager then I suppose anything is possible. I remind myself that I'm talking to somebody with mental illnesses that I don't understand, and I shift my tone.

"Well, that's really great. She sounds amazing, but you can't be nasty to people like you were at breakfast. You upset a lot of people."

He grunts in some sort of agreement. "Fine. Can you move from the TV now please? I got over five hundred million riding on this game."

My eyebrow arches at his fantasy. But I do as he asks – after all, he is a multi-millionaire, he deserves some respect.

Just as I go to walk off, Tom asks me if I'm a fan of Channing Tatum.

"Yeah, he's alright, I guess."

"Cool. He's my cousin. If he comes to visit me before I go home, I'll get him to come and say hello to you."

"That'll be nice, thanks," I answer. It's easier to play

along. As long as he has no more outbursts, he could be relatively harmless. Plus, the life he has made up sounds exciting. Maybe that is how he copes with whatever he is battling. Delulu is the solulu.

CHAPTER FIVE
WILL THE REAL NORMAN BATES PLEASE STAND UP?

I had my first session with Maddie today, she's nice. Young, friendly, easy to talk to. But if I'm really honest, I have no idea how much she can truly help me – I'm not sure she's ever had a panic attack in her life, and I always feel like the best therapists are the ones who can relate. But I open up and answer all her questions anyway because she is keen to help, and I really admire that.

Our first session wasn't too deep. She started by asking me how things were with my friendship group and my boyfriend. I told her they were fine. Honestly, looking back, I really don't know why I didn't tell her more of the truth. I could have opened up to her about the video and all the threats and I have no doubt she would have gone above and beyond to help me, but for some reason, I didn't tell her any of that. I kept it all to myself.

We then got onto the topic of my mum; she explained that Dr Pope wasn't sure if visits from my mum would be beneficial for me at this time since it appears that she is contributing to my illnesses. I didn't argue, although deep down I did feel a bit sad for Mum. She'd love to visit me – mostly for the drama, but still, I felt bad for her.

Later on, I got several new diagnoses added to my chart and I was allowed to read what they were before it got filed away.

1 – Severe anxiety disorder
2 – Panic disorder
3 – Extreme low self-esteem
4 – Borderline personality disorder

Number three surprised me and still does. It's true that back then I had truly little confidence, but I didn't know it was classed as a mental illness. Maybe it's not as such, could be more of a highlighted contributing factor. Number four blew my mind. I felt like I had just been given the worst diagnosis of all time.

I went back into the living room with my piece of paper looking for Katie. I found her in front of the TV watching *The Bodyguard* with Kevin Costner. I don't mean Kevin was there, I'm not hallucinating, don't worry, I mean the movie stars Kevin Costner. And Whitney Houston.

Anyway, Katie seemed like the least likely person to judge me, so I handed her the piece of paper and chewed my bottom lip whilst I waited anxiously for her to get to number four.

"None of those are that bad," she eventually announces.

A girl with a shaved head overhears us and comes over.

"But what about number four?" I ask.

Katie reads it out loud with a grin and shaved head girl bursts out laughing.

"That?! That's like the most common diagnosis ever, I wouldn't even worry. I think half the population have it," shaved girl says.

"Hey guys!" Katie calls out to the room. Jimbo stops shuffling his Pokémon cards and looks over, Lisa picks up her mug of tea and joins us on the sofa and a few other patients look over in our direction.

"Please raise your hands if your diagnosis sheet says you have a borderline personality disorder?"

And just like that, in unison, everyone in the room puts up their hand.

"Told ya!" Katie says with a smile. "It's all of us. It's a pretty standard diagnosis. I really wouldn't worry about it."

"She's right, and it's a pretty boring diagnosis to be fair. You sure you're not schizo or anything juicer?" Lisa weighs in.

"Nope. Just scared of life and everything in it apparently."

"You'll probably get better soon, leave this place and never come back. Unlike me. My mum calls me boomerang, I always come back." I eye Lisa's scars, saddened but curious to hear her story.

"Do you see your mum much?"

"Nah, she lives in Sheffield, she isn't going to come down to Kent to see me. She's probably high on something anyway with her moron boyfriend."

It's such a short sentence but it gives me a pretty clear picture of what Lisa's life looks like.

"What about your dad?" I ask, although I feel like I can predict the answer.

She shrugs. "Never met him." I nod – it's pretty much what I thought she'd say. I had a feeling, the way she walks around this place like she owns it, the confidence, the independence. This place is home to her. She's had to look after herself for a long time, that much I can see.

"Goodnight, ladies!" Jimbo interrupts as he stands to leave. He is wearing an extra hoodie this evening, so that makes five. A new record since my arrival.

"Oh, already Jimbo?" It's only 8:45pm.

"Yeah, my mum and dad are coming to visit me tomorrow. I can't wait. They're bringing me more Pokémon cards."

My face drops. "Oh, ok. Night then, Jim."

Jesus Christ. He thinks his parents are coming to see him. This is like Norman Bates in *Psycho*. This is worse than I thought – are these hallucinations? What if he gets *really* confused one night and thinks I'm his mum? Or even worse than that, what if he did something to their bodies? I swear if he pulls his dead mother out of his suitcase tomorrow and starts drinking tea with her, I'm going to faint. No cap. I will probably just pass away in fact.

"What are you looking so worried about?" Lisa interrupts my thoughts. "You'll sleep better tonight; the first night is always tough."

"Maybe, but it doesn't help that I'm opposite a parent killer."

"A what?"

I nod in the direction of Jimbo as he walks down the hall back to his bedroom. "You know, the axe?"

And with that, Lisa and Katie both throw their head back in fits of laughter.

"He didn't kill them!" Katie manages to inform me between fighting for breath.

I'm confused. I heard the story. It was pretty obvious what occurred once he got upstairs.

"He just smashed up his bedroom!" Lisa fills in the blanks. "He didn't hurt his parents; he just lost his marbles a bit and they called the police to restrain him and that's how he ended up here."

"So they're not dead?"

"No!" Katie giggles. "They're very much alive. They come and visit him regularly."

"I thought…" Oh my god, I feel like a right prick. In my defence, Miss Holland picked a *very* bad time to come in and end the conversation. I've spent the last twenty-four hours fearing Jimbo for no reason, well not *no* reason, he did trash his room with an axe which is still pretty intense, but he hasn't got blood on his hands and I'm taking that as a positive.

CHAPTER SIX

ARIANA, WHAT YOU DOING HERE?

Within days, I was in a new routine. My morning started at eight o'clock, then it was time to head down to the dining room for breakfast. After that, it could be therapy with Maddie, CBT therapy, exercise such as yoga, relaxation therapy with candles and hypnotherapy-style CDs to listen to and occasionally Art therapy. I really enjoyed Art therapy. I can't draw or paint very well, but I did make my mum and dad an ashtray back in year four which was the absolute bollocks if I do say so myself, so even if I just did my best to mimic that masterpiece, it was fun – there was music in the background, good vibes, everybody was chilled and usually got stuck in. I enjoyed it a lot. Sometimes, when the weather was decent, the staff would arrange for us to have a walk outside of the hospital too, usually to Knole Park, a nearby National

Trust property with deer roaming around. It was cutesy.

In the evenings, most of us would take it in turns to use the pay phone to ring home and catch them up on our days. I mostly phoned Dad of course. I phoned my cousin once, but he just laughed and sang Amy Winehouse's "Rehab" to me down the phone. I am starting to think singing down the phone is a trend in my family, what with Mum's renditions of ABBA hits and now this.

Movie time was usually the last thing we did together before going off to our rooms, although we had a list of films that were banned from being brought onto the ward, like *The Matrix*, *Number 23*, *The Butterfly Effect* and so on. Basically, movies that could make us overthink or confuse us. Or to sum up, a head fuck. I'm chuckling as I write this because I have *still* never watched a single *Matrix* movie because of this. They freaked me out by banning it and now I'm far too scared!

One night though, I couldn't sleep – out of the blue, I started feeling anxious. It started with the usual struggling to catch my breath properly or feeling as though the air wasn't going all the way into my lungs and then came the speedy heart rate. Worst of all, I had suddenly become consumed with an intense fear of impending doom – I was convinced something really bad was about to happen, but to me specifically, like a heart attack or a stroke. When you panic like that, you can't think straight. All your thoughts are muddled, you can't think logically and the intense feeling of being overwhelmed really consumes you. I remember getting a blackcurrant drink and going back to my bedroom to calm myself down. I couldn't taste the blackcurrant; I sipped at it and noticed my brain was so distracted with intense panic that I swear I couldn't taste anything. Which of course only added to my fear that I was having a stroke.

Loretta, the head nurse on duty, came by to do a routine check and saw me falling apart on my bed. I was shaking by this point, crying and rocking back and forth trying to somehow self-soothe.

Loretta took my blood pressure and it was 99/155. She said that if the 99 turned to 100 we'd have to go to A&E as per protocol. She seemed a little concerned but not overly. I knew A&E would be the worst place for somebody like me who has severe health anxiety. Loretta mentioned more tablets to stop the panic but that scared me even more – all these new tablets, what were they doing to me? What if they were making me worse? What if they were making my heart race and negatively affecting my health? All of these terrifying thoughts took over and I sobbed and pleaded with her that I couldn't do another new tablet.

"I'll come back and check your blood pressure again in ten minutes," she said instead. "Try to use any tools you learned in CBT."

I tried, but I couldn't think of a single thing. Or if I did, it certainly wasn't making any difference.

By this point, everybody else was likely asleep as the ward was so quiet; it was just me still awake, freaking out and completely hating that this was my life. How had I gone from watching some silly romcom movie to being in a severe episode of panic and anxiety? It was so frustrating – I shouldn't be like this, nothing scary had happened, I don't recall having been triggered or stressed out. So why was this happening? Why does this *always happen?* I am seventeen years old with so much enthusiasm towards life so why is it so hard to just live it? I hate this. I hate my life. I hate myself. I wish so bad sometimes that I could just fall asleep at night and never wake up.

"Chlo, do you want a cup of tea and to keep me company for ten minutes? I just got back from Egypt and I'm dying to tell somebody all about it."

A nurse I hadn't met before had popped her head into my room and interrupted my morbid thoughts. I hadn't met her before because obviously she's been on holiday. I love all things travel, I find it all so interesting to hear about people's visits aboard, so without hesitation, I followed her out into the kitchen and sat at one of the tables whilst she made us both a tea. I noticed the clock on the wall said 10:50pm. I hadn't been out of my room this late before. I still couldn't catch my breath very well, not without forcing a yawn, but I was here and Heather, the nurse freshly back from Egypt, was already relaying all of her adventures to me.

"Oh my god!" My jaw dropped open as Heather told me about one of her adventures– I had no idea the inside of those pyramids could be so tiny. "So what did you do?"

"Well, I managed," Heather continues. "But it

wasn't easy. I mean, I'm not usually a claustrophobic person but that was insane. Some parts I literally had to crawl on my hands and knees."

"No way!"

"Yes!" She laughs. "But it was so worth it. I had this constant eerie feeling when I was in there though, but I didn't mind, I just thought I'll never feel anything like this again, so just roll with it."

"Eerie, how?"

"I can't describe it; it just feels like the pyramids are still active. Weird I know and I'm not even superstitious! But it feels very much like that. Like you're being watched. Almost like you shouldn't really be there."

"Ooooh spooky! I love stuff like that, that's intriguing."

"If you love stuff like that, you should go one day. I think you'd find it fascinating."

The next time I happen to glance at the clock, I notice two things. Firstly, it is now half past eleven and secondly, I have been so absorbed listening to Heather describe what Egypt was like that I have become noticeably much calmer.

"80/135," Loretta announces when she comes back to do my blood pressure. "Much better!"

Heather just smiles. I realise this was part of her clever plan to distract me and I am so grateful – it worked! Forty-five minutes ago, I was convinced I was seriously ill, and I felt so terrified with those feelings that I even believed I'd be better off dead. Now, I'm feeling calm and wondering whether one day I could make it to

Egypt to see the pyramids. I head off to bed feeling comforted not only because Heather took the time to do that, but because I now know that I can calm down more quickly when my brain has something to focus on.

When I wake up the next morning, although I'm a little tired, I feel more relaxed knowing that last night's panic attack ended in a positive way. Before, the attacks would just go on until I'd be so physically and mentally exhausted that I'd eventually fall asleep. But not last night. Last night we managed to stop it in its tracks, and I feel better for it.

I spend some time alone in my room after breakfast, listening to garage music and writing in my diary.

My sixth day in this place and I feel like I could be turning a corner.

I feel brighter today, and I think it is because I haven't seen or spoken to college boyfriend now in almost a week. I didn't realise at the time, but I think he had a big hold over me. He controlled the way I thought and the way I saw myself. I remember when he came back from a family holiday in Arizona, and he told me he cheated on me with a gorgeous American girl. I cried. I felt so hurt. He told me I didn't look as good as her and I can only blame myself. After I cried for hours, he told me he didn't really cheat on me, but he thought I deserved the pain of thinking he did.

Apparently, this was because in the last two weeks whilst he was away, he didn't feel I texted him or kept in contact enough, or I was with friends too much, which showed disrespect. I needed to be reminded of what I could lose.

As I write this down, I know how incredibly damaging and toxic he is. I kick myself for not seeing it earlier. But I think he got inside my head and got me so confused. He once said he overheard my dad and stepmum talking about what a burden I am in their lives and how they're fed up with having me around. I believed that. But I have been vulnerable, I think I would have believed anything.

After all, he made me think the only person I could trust in this world was him.

As scared as I am to be in this place, I am grateful for the space it has given me to see that he is very bad for me. And I deserve better. I hope I never have to see him again now. I am a good person; I'm just going through a tough time.

"Chloe, you have visitors. I heard you had a rough night last night so you can spend time with them in your room if you prefer, instead of the visitors' lounge." I nod with a smile; Miss Holland is back on shift, and I think that is the nicest interaction we've ever had.

I hear my stepmum's boots click-clacking against the floor as she approaches my door. I tuck my diary away and turn off the music. I'm so relieved to see my dad and my stepmum and – oh. Jesus Christ. What is *he* doing here?

CHAPTER SEVEN

THOU SHALT NOT SWING FOR COLLEGE BOY

My dad had innocently brought college boy to visit me, thinking I'd really like the surprise. I don't. But unfortunately, only me and my new diary know how I feel about him, so it really isn't his fault. A huge part of me wants to tell my dad right here and right now about what being in this relationship has been like for me, then I'd sit back and watch my dad tear into him and make him walk home.

However, I don't do that. Even though I have come to understand that I wasn't the problem in this relationship, I still can't bring myself to speak on how foolish I have been and of course how incredibly embarrassing it is to know he has a video of me which he has been holding over my head. My poor dad has already had two heart attacks in his life, I really don't fancy giving him his third.

Instead, I paint a smile on my face and spend the next hour chatting to them. I avoid discussing anything too personal – the less college boy knows about me going forward the better. Eventually, my dad checks his watch which is usually his signal that he's about to head out. I use the opportunity to ask if I can speak to college boy alone before they leave. Of course, he agrees. He hugs me goodbye and he and stepmum head off to wait for Charles Manson – sorry, college boy – in the car.

I choose to break it off gently without bruising his ego and opt to avoid blame and give the excuse that I'm in a mental health hospital, which to be fair is a really good excuse. I tell him that he has been wonderful, but I need to look after myself for now. He buys it, of course he does, I don't think he'd ever imagine in a million years that he could be the problem. He momentarily looks like he could cry, which throws me off. But then he seems to accept it and agrees it is best. I thought he'd fight me so much more on this – he used to say that if I was to ever break up with him, he'd make my life hell and set fire to my house in the middle of the night whilst we all slept. I can only assume he is less bothered now because, let's face it, I'm boring. I'm not even allowed my phone, so he can't communicate with me, he can't force me to meet up with him, he can't threaten me with videos at three o'clock in the morning. For him, the fun is over anyway. Which is a massive relief.

I try not to dry heave as he gives me a hug goodbye. As I watch him disappear down the corridor and out the exit, I feel a massive weight fall from my shoulders. I definitely do not plan to be in another relationship any time soon.

CHAPTER EIGHT
CAN YOU NOT?

This week is one of the most challenging since I arrived here, and it all starts with Tom. So here I am, sitting in the visitors' lounge with my two friends from college when the emergency alarm is sounded and blares out on the speakers all around us. It is deafening. And quite frankly embarrassing. Both lads gawk into the hallway like somebody is going to suddenly appear naked, running around with their skid-marked pants on their head and chanting something about Jesus Christ our lord and saviour.

I assure them quickly that this is not an alarm because a patient is having some kind of psychotic break and that it indicates somebody has probably tried to hurt themselves, which I realise now was not much better and definitely not comforting.

I remember watching through the glass to the staffroom as one of the nurses checks the board to see which room has the alarm going off.

"ROOM 11!" she screams as half a dozen staff members rush towards it, including one of the head doctors; he is usually upstairs on the adult ward, but he appears at the double doors, frantic and desperate to quickly get to whoever needs his help.

I am so taken aback by all the commotion that it doesn't even register which patient belongs to room eleven at first. But then I realise: it's me. That emergency alarm is coming from my room.

"That's my room?" I say aloud because I can't make any sense of it and, although I am obviously safe and unharmed, I'm quite concerned about what is going on in my room.

Now the lads turn to look at me, eyes wide and jaws open like maybe I've gone a little crazy and actually there is currently a rabbit's head boiling in a pot in my bedroom or something. Their faces are a picture. It's like they are momentarily trying to figure out whether they should be scared of me or not.

Good news. It has nothing to do with me. Bad news. It has everything to do with Tom who, as we've seen, when he gets bored, likes to create a little drama.

"Tom, mate, do not touch anything else until you get showered off," the doctor says in an authoritative tone, his loud, firm voice travelling easily up the corridor to us.

Tom appears with his jeans unbuckled, hands in the air and a naughty smirk on his face.

I soon come to learn that the fucker has gone to my room and had a wank in my bed before pulling the alarm, for absolutely no other reason than to piss me off. My two friends go home double lively that day and I really can't blame them.

Even after my room has been cleaned, bedding changed, sanitised and exorcism performed, I still can't shake the feeling that my little safe space in this unit has been compromised, and I no longer feel as settled as I had. Cheers Tom. You know that episode of *Friends* where Joey gets a job working with Chandler and he makes up an entire fake family to everyone Chandler works with, then on the spot he makes up fake pregnancies and fake children too? Well, I feel like doing the same with Tom's fantasy girlfriend and completely fucking with him. Maybe I'll accidentally hit her with my car. Oh no, wait, I just did. Oh, and his beloved Portsmouth FC? Relegated. They are so bad at football now that even ten-year-old kids in the park don't want to play them. I feel a bit better now.

After Tom *came* and ruined my week, literally, I have a new challenge ahead of me. My mum is finally coming to visit, and I have no idea how it is going to go. She is coming with my sister which I think will make it a little less intense, but still, my mum has a tendency to be a bit like Tom – not a masturbation fiend, but she would certainly play up for the drama given half the chance. And a mental health unit where her daughter had been admitted? And a string of trained medical staff who would listen to her rant? Perfect place.

***

A few days later and I'm starting to feel somewhat better about being in my room when I hear my mum's voice out in the hallway.

"My daughter is here, Chloe?"

"Ah yes, room eleven," I hear.

Now I already know that drunk Carol is a mix between the devil and an ABBA tribute act. But what I haven't seen much of the last few years is sober Carol. She's not usually much better to be fair and I am certainly apprehensive about how the next couple of hours are going to pan out. Which version of my mum am I going to get?

As suspected, my sister joins in with the visit and they bring goodies with them, like chocolate and magazines. Mum also brought me a book called *The Zodiac Killer*. Bless her, I'm not allowed to watch *The Matrix* so a psychological thriller about a real-life serial killer will likely be off limits too. But I nod and smile and tell her I appreciate it.

The first question Mum asks me isn't about how I'm doing, or what the food is like in this place. No, she asks me what the girl with the shaved head is in here for.

"Oh, you met her then?"

"She said hello when we came in. Why has she done that to herself? Oh my god, is she dying? Is it cancer?"

I shrug. "No, she just didn't want hair anymore."

"Really? But she could be so pretty with hair. She must be deeply disturbed."

I can't help but roll my eyes – the gossip and drama picking has begun. I know we are all partial to a bit of gossip, but my mum's style of gossiping has always felt particularly unkind.

"And what's with the young lad wearing four jumpers?" Her tone continues to be judgemental.

Ah, Jim. I feel particularly protective of Jim, he is the only one in this place with a very different type of mental illness, he isn't as obviously anxious or depressed as the rest of us, in fact he presents himself as always being so happy, enthusiastic and excitable. Just like a little boy. Obviously, the excessive wearing of jumpers tells us different, but I like Jimbo – in a place that can feel very dark, he is a bright smile.

"Makes him feel safe," I mumble. I'm getting too wound up to speak at a normal volume. I can feel myself detaching already and she's only just arrived. It's not really my place to answer why everybody else is in here and worst of all, she hasn't even asked why *I'm* in here. I haven't lived with her in three years, so she has no idea what it has been like or what a battle I face at night. I really thought she would have asked by now.

"Has anyone tried to run away yet?"

"Sometimes."

"What happens if they run away?"

"Usually, they are found by staff or the police bring them back."

"And what's the girl with the missing teeth in here for? Who did that to her?"

"I fell over and smashed my face against the pavement," Lisa surprises me by answering. She's stood in the doorway, arms folded across her chest, watching my mum with a smirk on her face. I'm not sure how long she's been there.

"Sorry, I know it's a boring answer."

My mum is struggling to form a sentence to respond when Lisa continues.

"And I'm here because my mum has been an addict most of her life and it messed me up. I've tried to kill myself half a dozen times, I have attempted to run away from here three times, once I was successful and made it down to the train station before the police brought me back. Also, the girl with the shaved hair was trying to make herself ugly. Something to do with her uncle. Jim is probably autistic, but you should probably just worry about Chloe, since that's why you're here."

And with that she stuffs her hands into her pockets and walks off. Leaving my mum momentarily speechless.

"You should avoid her Chloe; you can tell a mile off she's trouble."

Troubled I wanted to say. Like most of the people in here, they aren't trouble. But troubled. There is a huge difference, and the most important one is that none of them are behaving like this on purpose.

"What does your *dad* think of her?" she spits out *dad* like the word is venomous.

"I don't think he thinks anything. He doesn't ask me about anyone."

Her lips curl up in dismay like that was the wrong answer to give.

"Anyway, I was thinking," she says, finally changing the subject as she sits on the edge of my bed. "What's your therapist called? The main one who makes all the decisions?"

"Dr Pope."

"Yeah, him. I think we need to call him in, and you need to explain to him that in order to get better you ideally need me and your *father* to sit in a room together and all of us to discuss your treatment plan and how you're going to get better."

I try to take a deep breath, but the air doesn't feel like it goes all the way back into my lungs, I think they call it air hunger. But in easy terms, it basically means I'm growing anxious.

My mum and dad haven't been in the same room for three years. My dad has an injunction against her and at one point he had one in place for me as well. There isn't a person my mum hasn't dragged into the crossfire in order to hurt my dad these last few years, including my elderly nan. My mum would write her letters being incredibly spiteful about my dad and even my nan's other children. She'd write things like *'What sort of woman raises a spineless man who leaves his wife of twenty years?'* It was vile. Especially since my nan was probably one of the kindest and most gracious people to ever walk this earth.

She has told my school that I died, sent funeral brochures to our house with our names on the gravestones, she has threatened to kill herself to me in 3am phone calls to get her way and don't even get me started on what she did to my cat. And somehow, she still has the audacity to think that firstly, she could have any positive input into my recovery and secondly, that anyone would want to sit in a room with her after what she has put us through.

But this isn't about me. It is never about me. This is about Mum seizing an opportunity to get my dad on his own. This is about what *she* wants.

CHAPTER NINE

GRIFF

We may as well discuss the cat. There are a few things in life that over time I have learned to forgive and there are some things that hurt so bad, I know I never will.

My cat being one of them.

I was around nine years old when my dad finally gave in and said that we could bring our first pet into the home. I'd always wanted a cat and before I knew it, one very rainy day, Dad drove us to a rescue centre to find a cat to rehome.

I vividly remember the first time I saw Griff; he was an all-black cat and the only one who was sitting in the rain. All the other cats had the sense to go indoors for shelter. But not Griff. I remember my dad stroking him and laughing.

"You're a bit dopey aren't you, silly boy," my dad said, smiling. Yep, I was sold, that was the cat for us.

Griff was roughly four years old and was found in some bin in Wales. I'm not quite sure how he ended up in a rescue centre in Kent but here he was. Within a couple of weeks, after a home check and some paperwork, we were finally bringing Griff home. And what an adventure that turned out to be. I quickly learned that Griff was not like any regular cat – he was a complete and utter psychopath. I can only assume now that the reason he was sitting in the rain that day is because all the other cats had the good sense to not let him in.

Griff sat in a cardboard cat carrier in the backseat of my dad's car for all of thirty seconds before his paw came flying through the roof like Mike Tyson punching a paper bag – and then he was free. He ran around the car absolutely scaring the shit out of nine-year-old me and when we got him home and settled, he was worse.

Griff absolutely detested people walking up the stairs. It would wind him up big time and he'd have no choice but to chase you and, if he caught you, you got a sharp scratch to the back of your legs. Griff also didn't like people standing next to him and breathing, as I realised quite soon when he stuck his claws into the side of my neck simply for being too close. And Griff, above all else, absolutely hated the white doves that were in our back garden. They weren't ours. Well, they were, I guess – they just came with the house when we moved in. The previous owners had built a ten-foot-tall bird house and kept a dozen white doves and didn't take them when they left. Griff would catch them, not even eat them, but remove their heads and leave their headless bodies on our doorstep. See. Total psycho.

Despite all this, Griff somewhat mellowed in time. He loved a cuddle and would sit on my lap for hours; he had the loudest purr, and he soon found comfort sleeping at the end of my bed each night. He was playful, full of character and brought me a lot of happiness.

My mum wasn't really an animal person and she didn't care for cats or dogs. I think that was mostly because she wasn't an affectionate person. She didn't really hug me and my sister as we grew up, so she definitely wasn't going to do that for an animal. So I was really surprised when, on the day Dad announced he was leaving, she said I couldn't take the cat.

She looked me dead in the eye as if I was the evillest person for even suggesting it.

"Nice Chlo, you want to take the only company I have?" she said, intending to guilt trip me. And it worked. In hindsight, I felt awful – Mum was getting to stay in the family house like she wanted, but it was a large five-bed, three-storey detached house. It was a lot for anyone to be rattling around in on their own. I didn't want her to be lonely, I didn't want her to feel any pain from this. So I gave Griff a kiss and reluctantly said goodbye to him.

As the weeks turned into months, I asked Dad a few times whether he thought I could bring Griff into our new home yet, but he kept saying it was best not to upset my mum with it and just to sit tight and wait until the house sale had gone through. Once she moved into her new home, maybe she'd be happy for me to take Griff.

One Friday afternoon, I'd gotten off the bus from school and was heading to my mum's house. It wasn't too often that I spent time with her – after all, she drank a lot, she got angry and she seemed to want to argue with me about my dad. But that weekend, I was making the effort. I had phoned a few days before to tell her and she seemed excited, but when I arrived at the house, nobody was home. I suddenly realised my phone was dead; it was getting dark and I needed to get Dad to pick me up, otherwise I'd be stuck sitting in my garden until Sunday when he collected me.

I was really starting to panic when a friend and her boyfriend turned up to knock for me. I asked him if he could climb up onto the conservatory and through my bedroom window to let me in. He did. He accidentally broke an ornament on my windowsill but at least I was in. I could grab my other charger and text Dad.

Within minutes, Griff appeared. He looked thin and lacking in energy. He meowed so loudly and eagerly that I quickly realised he was desperate for food. I went into the kitchen and saw his food bowl; it was disgusting with bits of old food caked onto it. I checked the cupboards and there was one half tin left with a fork shoved into it. It hadn't been covered properly and had gone all dry. It didn't look like he'd been fed recently. I reluctantly fed him the last of the can, feeling guilty that it definitely wasn't appetising. Luckily, I found some chicken and ham in the fridge and added that into his bowl too. He ate every last scrap.

When Dad picked me up, I told him how Griff

looked. He said we couldn't just *take* Griff because things were getting really ugly in the divorce court and Mum might claim it as theft. Instead, he said he'd call his solicitor with proof that Griff was bought for me and then maybe we could work something out.

However, as I walked out of school on Monday afternoon and headed back home, my mum rang my phone.

"Chloe, have you been in my house? I won't get mad, just tell me."

I was instantly confused. "Yes? I was there for a while but then Keeley said you'd gone away for the weekend, so I got Dad to pick me up."

"So you're the one who smashed my ornament?"

"No, a friend climbed in the window and accidentally knocked it off."

"Right. Ok. I thought someone had broken in."

I wondered what sort of burglar breaks in, takes absolutely nothing and then feeds the family cat.

She hung up the phone when I mentioned Griff.

I'd been home for about two hours when a police officer came to the door to arrest me for breaking and entering. I've never been more terrified. I remember my dad saying this couldn't possibly be a charge because he owned the house, and had given me permission to enter when I needed to.

According to the law though, when someone has vacated the house for long enough, even if they own it, they lose the right to come and go and so the person who resides there full time has the right to press charges. And she did. My mum pressed charges against her now fifteen-year-old daughter for entering her own childhood home.

Thankfully, once the police officer understood the story, he agreed that it was ridiculous. He didn't put me into the police car in the end and allowed my dad to drive me to the station and sit with me whilst I had to listen to Mum's statement full of lies and deceit. I was let off with a caution, but I am sure it stayed somewhere on my file for a long time. I didn't want to stress my dad out any further, so I behaved as if I wasn't too phased and was taking it all in my stride, but I cried myself to sleep that night.

As you can imagine, I didn't see or speak to my mum for a long time after that. Eight months later and the once family home was ready for viewings and very shortly after that, my mum found a semi-detached three-bedroom house in Pembury, Kent, to move into. Our family home now just stood empty, bricks and mortar filled with good and bad memories.

It was around two weeks after Mum moved out when the first couple actually went round with the estate agent for a viewing. Following that appointment, the estate agent phoned my dad with a serious concern and my heart broke.

My mum had vacated the house two weeks ago and had left Griff behind. She didn't let anyone know that she was doing that, she just did it. The cat that she was adamant I couldn't have had been left to starve. Most cats as we know are really resilient and will often hunt for their food, but Griff didn't stand a chance – he was locked in with no way out. He was extremely skinny and close to death. My dad drove us straight across, and the sight was unforgiveable. Areas of the home smelt strongly of urine and faeces because Griff couldn't get outside. He was so skinny I could see his little ribs poking through his balding fur and my once fierce psychopathic cat looked weak and feeble. He rubbed his head against my legs with such excitement to finally see me again, but it was a struggle for him to maintain that energy.

I have never felt so guilty in all my life as I did then. An innocent animal got caught up in the messy mind games of my mum. I sobbed when I saw him, I just kept saying sorry. I think the worst part was when he started purring again, I felt like I didn't deserve that purr. The poor thing had been so neglected and yet he was just so happy I was there now.

Later that evening, a woman came to collect Griff and I had to say my final goodbyes. Dad said that he was really weak and needed nursing back to health by someone who knew what she was doing and that this was the best thing we could offer him now. Looking back, I wonder if that was really the case or whether Griff just wasn't going to survive and my dad wanted to spare me any more hurt.

When I asked my mum sometime later why she did that to Griff, she said she couldn't get him to her new house. And made out it was my fault for leaving her to navigate a divorce and move house by herself. She showed no remorse.

That of course was just an excuse. She did it because it would hurt me and hurting me meant hurting my dad. And she strived for that.

It feels nice to have a chapter in here just for Griff and I know that may sound silly, but he was a rescue cat who was meant to have a second chance, and he deserves to be remembered.

I know the saying "hell hath no fury like a woman scorned", but I didn't ever think that my mum had *this* side to her. That she could be so cold and callous.

CHAPTER TEN
ONE MENTY B PLEASE

I try to tell my mum, no. I try to explain that Dr Pope wouldn't think that getting her and Dad in the same room was a particularly good idea right now and that it's still early days. Which has truth to it anyway – I have only just begun my sessions with Maddie, I'm only just getting into a better sleep routine, but the anxiety is still very much there. They are small steps but they're my steps. Even Dad isn't involved in anything right now, the hospital just calls him to deliver updates on how my days have gone.

I don't want to sit in a room and allow her to use me as a pawn against my dad. I don't want to watch her lie to Dr Pope's face as she makes up reasons as to how it's everyone else's fault that she had to do all the things she did.

Plus, I can't even bring myself to relive all the hurt she has caused me. I don't want to have to tell Dr Pope that I'm scared that I'll struggle to get a job because I may have 'breaking and entering' on my record. Or that I'm blaming myself every day for Griff. Or that I am terrified that my dad, who has heart disease, won't be able to cope with the stress she has caused.

My head starts running wild with all these thoughts and fears and my breathing becomes fast and shallow. My vision is blurry, and I try to blink it away, but the next time I open my eyes, my mum has a marker pen and she's writing a message for my dad on the whiteboard. Of course she is, she's ignoring my pleas. And worst of all, I can't even wipe it off because she's used the wrong pen, she's used a fucking permanent marker.

We must work together for Chloe. We must forget the past and move forward. Call me asap so we can arrange to meet. For Chloe.

I just wanted my mum to visit me today and be more of the mum I needed. Her first visit and she hasn't asked me a single question about myself, and she is *still* obsessed with Dad. My wellbeing is still not her priority. Her teenage daughter is in a mental health unit, and it hasn't been enough of a wake-up call to stop her being so fucking selfish.

I storm out of my bedroom and into the arms of Heather. "Please," I say through the catch in my throat, "can you tell my mum that she has to leave now?"

She doesn't even question it or hesitate. "Of course, visits are on your terms only."

I can't bear to watch so I run off to the kitchen to get a glass of water and I try to distract myself from the panic setting in by thinking about five things I can see, four things I can feel, three things I can hear, two things I can smell.

Of course, that's practically impossible when one of the things I can hear is Mum creating a drama in the hallway. I look through the window and see she isn't mad but rather seems to be forcing back tears, saying that this is because my dad has caused a divide between us. Then she starts saying how mentally ill she is. She starts listing off all the things wrong with her and Heather just nods politely but keeps one hand on her back as she leads her to the exit. She wants everyone to feel sorry for her.

I can still hear her going on, but now she's talking more about my dad, about how he left her after twenty years of marriage, about what an amazing wife she was and didn't deserve this. Eventually, her voice fades until I can't hear her at all but when I return to my room and see her message to my dad in permanent marker on my wall, I just flip. All this built-up anger that I didn't know I had just pours out of me, and I don't know what to do with it. In the past I would release it by cutting my arms a bit, nothing major, but enough to draw blood, it used to feel like a relief, like I was letting it all out somehow.

But I can't do that here, so I start throwing things. My CD player first but then I'm kicking my chest of drawers over and stamping on the wood. I'm throwing my chair across the room and trying to smash my window. It's all a blur really until Heather comes bursting into my room.

"Stop, Chloe! Otherwise, you'll have to be

restrained." I stop, mostly because there's not much in this room and I've pretty much already attacked everything I can. Oh, and I saw Tom getting restrained once, it was hilarious but also looked a bit rough, so I don't want that for me.

I end up slumped on the floor next to my bed, sitting in the mess I created with Heather who has her arms around me.

"We can stop your mum visiting again for now, if you think that would be better?" I nod, tears falling down my cheeks.

I've barely got my breath back when, to my surprise, my dad steps into my room. His eyes are wide in shock as he takes in the scene in front of him. It's not like me and he knows it. I'm rarely an angry person, I don't even recognise myself right now, I just feel embarrassed. Heather, as amazing as she is, stands up quickly and starts picking things up off the floor; my dad and stepmum help her. It doesn't take long, and nothing is actually broken. Well, maybe my CD player. I can tell Dad is about to ask what has happened when he sees my mum's handwriting on the whiteboard.

"When did she write this?"

"Carol left ten minutes ago," Heather answers for me. "I'll let you have some privacy."

My dad puts his hands in his pockets, occasionally staring at mum's message and then back to the floor. I can see he is trying to process it and trying to figure out what to say.

"You can't be trashing the place though, Chlo.

They're trying to help you here and the last thing you want is to be kicked out."

"I know," I agree. I feel silly already.

"Plus, I already spoke to Dr Pope about what he recommends, and he definitely doesn't think that some kind of family therapy like your mum wants would be the right move. He thinks she needs to get her own therapy first and I agree."

Dad spends the next hour doing what he does best, trying to make a joke with me and lighten my mood. It works.

That evening, I was looking forward to a movie night with Katie. She usually stuck on a romcom before bed. *The Bodyguard* was her favourite, but I knew tonight she had mentioned watching *Bridget Jones's Diary*. Heather had even said she was going to bring in some popcorn for us. It sounded like the perfect ending to a crappy day, plus I knew Katie was feeling anxious today as well; it felt like we could both use getting lost in a decent film.

I didn't realise though that at some point during my own commotion, Katie had managed to gain access to the medicine cupboard, grabbed a concoction of pills and gone to her room and taken every single one. Apparently, she was in therapy with Maddie when she collapsed and was now in hospital. We didn't have an update; we didn't even know if she was awake or fighting for her life.

She had been smiling this morning. I had noticed her breathing was shallow and I knew she was a bit anxious, but she was smiling. To me, she was having a good day. But at some point, since then, she had decided to try and take her own life.

When Loretta comes in for her evening shift, she is instantly surrounded by all the patients as they push for information. Even Tom hovers close by and Tom usually doesn't care about anything.

"She's really, really poorly at the moment guys. It's all I can say. As soon as I know more, you'll know."

Tears fill Jimbo's eyes as he paces the hallway anxiously before disappearing to his room.

"Someone had better be held accountable for leaving the fucking cupboard unlocked!" Lisa cuts in, visibly agitated.

"Yes, Lisa." Loretta's hands are raised as if to calm her. "We are of course looking into what has gone wrong."

"Here," Jim says as he reappears clutching a Pokémon card. "It's really rare and going to be worth a lot of money one day my dad said, but will you give it to Katie? Maybe it will make her smile again and then she can come back here."

"That's really sweet Jim, but I know Katie will want you to hold onto that and look after it for her," Loretta answers.

"Yeah. Ok. I could do, couldn't I? Yes, I'll keep it safe. Because she'll be home really soon won't she Loretta? Like, tomorrow?"

"Not tomorrow, Jim."

"Oh. Then Wednesday?"

"Probably not, but I'll keep you all updated, ok?"

I can tell between Lisa's agitation and Jimbo's restlessness that Loretta is concerned this will rile up everyone before bed. It goes like this sometimes, people here struggle to process things and it causes everyone to become unsettled.

I think maybe we could all use a film after all, anything to distract us a bit would be good right now.

"Jim, will you watch *Bridget Jones's Diary* with me?"

"Oh ok. But is it alright to watch someone else's diary?"

"Yeah," I say with a smile as he follows me into the living room. "It's not like a real diary, it's all pretend but it's good." Thankfully, Lisa follows, even Tom; a few of the others go back to their rooms but for the most part everybody is a lot calmer.

CHAPTER ELEVEN

ALEXA, PLAY "LOCKED UP" BY AKON.

It was a strange feeling as the weeks went by. I soon learned that being cut off from the outside world wasn't as bad as I first thought it would be. Without my phone and the internet, I didn't have access to social media so I couldn't see any hate, drama or gossip. I couldn't see the mainstream news and learn about new scary things that were happening. Crimes committed. Terrorist threats. I had no clue whether there was another new war brewing somewhere in the world, I didn't know if the government had done something to upset people again, I didn't know if Russia was threatening anybody – I didn't even know if Katie Price had a new husband. All I knew was the bubble that I was in with the people I was with. I knew my new routine, I filled my day with therapy, art therapy, music, meditation, three good meals, reading and good conversation, whether that be with fellow patients or staff members. And it was easy, but most importantly it was freeing.

My mind wasn't plagued with worries about things that I couldn't change, or anxious about negativity online. Everything was stripped away and it made my days feel simpler. Of course, it wasn't perfect. I was still unwell, we all were, but at least these were issues that were in front of me and that I could deal with, instead of online or around the world that I had no control over.

It's strange, isn't it, how our availability was expected to change when mobile phones came along? Back in the day, you rang someone's house phone if you wanted to chat and if they weren't home, you just waited for them to get back to you. That was kind of the unwritten rule and etiquette of communication. Now, I was realising that our society was way more impatient than that and certainly far more expecting. If you don't reply instantly to a text message, you are almost always nudged with a "??" And people don't just communicate via phone call or text now – no, you can be contacted in several different ways on various different apps. Trying to keep up can be exhausting, not to mention overwhelming.

I hadn't realised how 'available' I had made myself. How I never switched my phone off and silenced the outside noise. I was quickly learning that there were many positives of not being glued to my phone – and my mind not being so clouded was one of them.

The only downside was that the hospital had become a little too much like a safe haven and the thought of going out into the world again scared me. This weekend coming I was going to be having my first day out of here since I had been admitted two weeks ago. Dad was picking me up and the plan was to spend a day in London. On paper, it sounded fun – window shopping, strolling around and then stopping for a nice lunch somewhere.

But my mind was already racing with thoughts:

What if it's really busy?

I can't go too far away from the car because the car feels safer than being out on the street.

Will Dad know not to park the car too far away?

Where will my exits be? Will they be easy to get to?

What if I freak out in front of everyone?

I don't usually cope with restaurants, what if it's like that this weekend and I can't enjoy my lunch and I have to leave. It'll be a waste of Dad's money.

How far will the restaurant be from the car, exactly?

It's so important that I'm not far from the car.

Maybe we can just stay in the car.

When the day arrives, I sign my little day release form and tick a box which states I am not suicidal or in the mood to hurt anyone. There isn't a box that says *may freak out if the car is parked too far away*, so I just sign, smile and head on out with my dad and my stepmum.

And actually, once we are in the car, the sun shining through the windows and warming my face, radio on in the background, I quickly relax. It feels strange to be away from the hospital but actually so nice to be enjoying the sun and seeing something more than corridors and walls.

Dad is careful to park the car somewhere easily accessible and central. We don't need to walk far from it either because we find a Garfunkel's nearby and decide that has to be the restaurant of choice. Dad always took us to Garfunkel's at the airport before holidays when we were kids, so it's definitely a spot with good memories.

We enjoy a nice lunch together under the late May sun. I don't get nearly as anxious as I thought I might – it still isn't a breeze to be out and in a social setting by any means, but I manage to eat the majority of my lunch *and* maintain an actual conversation, which is a huge win.

This isn't just the first time I have been out since being admitted, but probably the first time in a good ten months or so. I had been so cooped up in my bedroom the last several months that I had lost any hope that I might be able to do this again. But I have done it. Today's a good day.

I head back into the hospital with a spring in my step when Dad drops me off. Today has given me hope. Hope that maybe one day I'll be more like a regular teenager and be able to go to restaurants and sleepovers and days out again without becoming terrified.

My jaw drops when the first person I see is Katie sitting on the sofa watching a movie, her legs curled up under a blanket. She is yellow. Like Bart Simpson yellow, I've never seen anything like it in my life.

She gives me a small smile like she's nervous. I'm

not sure what about, perhaps everyone's reaction to seeing her, or maybe she's even embarrassed. I don't know, but I instantly plop myself down on the opposite sofa and smile back. Just so happy to see her alive.

"I heard you got to go out today. How did it go?" I love that the first thing Katie asks is how my day went. She knew I was nervous about the idea of days out from before. But let's not ignore the big fat elephant in the room.

"Katie, how are *you?* What the hell happened? When did you get back?"

"About an hour ago. I don't really know what happened, it's all such a blur. I just saw my opportunity and took it."

My eyes flit up and down her body, taking in her frail and jaundiced appearance. It hurts my heart.

"I didn't know… I didn't know you wanted to die?" I whisper.

"I didn't know either. But I saw the tablets and just thought I could slip away today and that would be it. No more anxiety, no more panic attacks, no more being so scared all the time. I'm tired. Aren't you tired, Chloe?"

I'm nodding before I even have time to think about it. Am I tired? I think back to the last few years. I phoned my dad once to pick me up from college boy's house at three o'clock in the morning because I was so anxious and couldn't sleep. A boyfriend before that had to wake his mum up in the middle of the night because of the same problem. They lived in Brighton so I couldn't exactly ask Dad to pick me up from there at that time.

But I remember her being really kind and lighting these lavender scented candles and telling me to concentrate on the smells as a distraction.

I remember going to Thorpe Park with friends and having to call myself a taxi after forty minutes because I was *so* anxious. I was dizzy, my heart was racing and I was convinced I was passing out. It cost like a hundred pounds to get home, and my two friends were so angry at me for leaving. One of them didn't talk to me again. She said it was attention seeking.

I think back to all the times I have begged my dad to take me to hospital, even though it terrifies me there, but I have been so convinced of being really ill with a serious illness that I made myself believe that without medical help I'd die.

I think back to being sixteen years old and my stepmum changing my bed sheets because I'd wet myself again in my sleep because I was that scared of nighttime.

I think about all the times I've had to say no. No to that party, no to that meal out, no to my best friend's birthday sleepover, no to my boyfriend's mum's fiftieth, no to trying out that new club, no to going to watch that new movie at the cinema, no to that concert, no to that girl's holiday. Hell, how about no to a simple trip to ASDA.

So yes. I am so fucking tired.

"I'm tired. Exhausted even. But all the while we have hope, that's what we should cling on to. Because what if it does get better than this? We just feel like it won't, but that doesn't mean the better days aren't out there."

"I just want to wake up and go outside like a normal person without feeling like I can't breathe," she croaks.

"There is every chance we can have days like that. What if one day, ten years from now, we are married, on a holiday, sipping sangria and watching the sun set? We might have a moment then where we think back to this conversation and think about how we held on because of hope. And we'll think about how wrong we once were, because it does get better. We'll have proof of that."

"I don't know…"

"Ok. What if when we are older, it's a series of good and bad days. Maybe that's more realistic. In ten years' time, the bad days are still there but what if the good days are making it all worth it?"

That seems to grab Katie's attention more. She looks at me now with more hope in her eyes than she had five minutes ago.

"I hope there are more good days than bad," she eventually adds.

"Me too. But we won't know if we give up now. You're not going to, you know, try *again* are you?"

She laughs and nods towards one of the nurses sitting in the corner with a book.

"Couldn't anyway, I'm on one-to-one for the foreseeable future."

Thank God for that I think to myself.

"And anyway, I'm sure I died for a minute, and it was really boring."

"Good. I'm glad. In fact, if you had died, I'd like to think you were sent to Hell where it's just a dark room with Jimbo explaining his Pokémon cards over and over again." We burst out laughing and right on cue Jimbo walks in from his day out with his parents.

"Katie!" he shouts with all his usual excitement and enthusiasm. "Did you know you're yellow? Like really yellow?"

We both instantly giggle.

"Yes Jim," Katie laughs, "I realise I'm a bit yellow."

"Not a bit! You're *really* yellow. Like Pikachu."

This childlike, unfiltered Jim is my favourite. I'm growing more and more fond of him every day.

"Would you like a cup of tea Katie? I can make you one, well, I need Loretta to come and watch me because Mum said I can't use the kettle until I'm eighteen."

I smile. "I'll make it Jim. Why don't you sit with Katie and tell her about Pikachu's strengths and weaknesses, since she looks so much like him."

"Yes, I will! Did you know he has Gigantamax power and can become supersize?"

I pretend I don't see Katie's secret middle finger jokingly aimed in my direction as Jim gets comfortable under the blanket.

Suddenly, over the noise of the kettle boiling, I hear shouting and screaming.

"Oh yeah…" Katie calls to me across the room. "I was supposed to tell you something happened with Lisa."

"DO NOT *FUCKING* TOUCH ME," I hear loud

and clear from the corridor. "LET ME OUT NOW OR I'LL STAB MYSELF WITH THIS FORK."

I hurry out into the hallway to see Lisa trying her hardest to get past Jake, one of the healthcare assistants. He's about six feet though, a rugby player and built like a brick shithouse. I don't fancy Lisa's odds.

"What happened?" I whisper to Katie from the doorway.

"Her mum was supposed to come down tomorrow to take her out for the day, but she cancelled earlier. And she lost it. She's been like this since I got back."

Lisa stomps past us, seemingly giving up on trying to run out the exit. Next thing we hear is her furniture being thrown against the wall. Minutes after that, she reappears with blood dripping down her arms – she has somehow managed to find something sharp enough to self-harm with. It's chaos and the staff have no choice but to send us back to our rooms.

Nights like this are hard. Hearing another patient having a meltdown is a mixture of upsetting and scary. Knowing the staff are flapping around and stressed makes the atmosphere twice as intense.

All you can do is sit in your room and pass the time reading a book or doing a crossword puzzle. And you know that if the patient doesn't quieten down by lights out, they'll be given something to calm them down, which isn't much nicer because mentally they're still in distress, they just can't physically do anything about it.

Eventually, it does grow quieter out there. One of the nurses comes by and shines a torch through my window to check in and tell me it's time to turn in. I fall asleep thinking about Katie and about our chat earlier, but my very last thought is how sad I feel for Lisa. I can't imagine being here without my dad supporting me. I hate her mum for making her like this tonight, for allowing her own child to go to bed thinking that she isn't loved enough by the one person who should do it unconditionally.

CHAPTER TWELVE
NEW KIDS ON THE BLOCK

As usual, we are woken early, get dressed and head down to the dining room for breakfast. Lisa is quiet – she seems ok, just quiet. When it comes to her mum though, Lisa doesn't tend to share too much. And nobody pushes her on it either.

Katie is obviously still yellow at breakfast which Jim points out several times before going on to apologise to the cook for her appearance in case it is reminding her of the kids' programme *Bananas in Pyjamas*. My favourite part is when he refers to Katie as being a silly billy because she ingested too many tablets. Like it was a completely innocent mistake.

I love watching the adult patients engage with Jim at breakfast; they've all gotten to know him – after all, he is the only six-foot teenager in this place who behaves like he is six years old. Most people high five him and smile when he's around. He has that influence.

By the time we are finishing up with breakfast, even Lisa has managed to smile a bit more, thanks to Jim comparing Katie to a lemon.

When we arrive back onto the ward, the energy is strange. We can't access the living room because there is a new patient in there who is being shown around and another new patient, a female, will be arriving later. Two patients in one day is quite unusual.

I can easily feel that the staff are way more tense than I've seen them. It's usually quite relaxed here; sure, I've had my meltdown, Lisa's had hers, Tom's a serial wanker and Katie's tried to off herself, but apart from that, we are easy. For the most part, the staff have our respect, most of them have become our friends. I'd personally be lost without Heather and although Lisa gives Loretta a bit of lip, they have a good bond. Loretta has known Lisa for many years.

But today, the new patient seems to have everyone behaving differently, almost on edge.

"Was everyone like this when I arrived?" I ask Katie but Lisa answers instead.

"No." Her voice is full of concern and suspicion. "It's never been like this before. I'm going to speak to Loretta."

If anyone can get Loretta to give us an idea about what is actually going on, then it'll be Lisa.

I watch the man in the lounge being shown around; occasionally, he throws his head back like an involuntary tick. His face is stern and serious. Not at all nervous or shy like I was when I arrived, but angry and unkind.

He walks with a slight limp and uses a brown walking stick to help him. He must be eighteen, he looks old enough to be upstairs with the adults, but he can't be since he's here.

Suddenly, he turns and locks eyes with me and clamps down on his jaw in some weird passive aggressive way. If it's meant to intimidate me, it works. His aura, his dark stare, the way he works his jaw as he watches me. He's successfully made me scared. I'm uncomfortable.

"Loretta won't tell me much, but he is high risk. It took four men to restrain him to get him here and in his last place he was *difficult.*"

"So he could hurt us?" Katie whispers to Lisa.

"Yep. Us, the staff, anyone who gets in his way, I guess. Don't be scared though, I'm here and I won't let him hurt anyone."

I'm sure Lisa thinks that this is going to reassure us, but it really doesn't. I can hardly hide behind her for the rest of my time here and as much as I am sure Lisa can hold her own, I'm unconvinced that she'll come out on top against this guy.

"Have you ever had anyone be violent here before?"

Lisa thinks about it for a minute. "Well no, not really. I mean people can have violent outbursts, sure, but I've never really known someone to turn up and have everyone on edge."

Oh great, just fucking great.

Jim approaches us with a huge smile on his face. "Did you hear? We have a new person joining today, I'm so excited. Can't wait to say hello."

I'm suddenly filled with concern and with a need to protect Jim. I feel scared that he could get himself hurt. It is Jim after all, he doesn't exactly sense danger from people.

"Jim, I think maybe you should just stay away from him for now. Let me talk to him first," Lisa says.

"Oh, but I like to help people feel settled. I could show him my Pokémon cards…"

"Jim, did you learn about stranger danger when you were at primary school?" I interrupt and he chews his bottom lip as he tries to recall.

"Ah yes!" His finger points up as if the memory just popped into his head. "Stranger danger is that you don't talk to strangers and if they try to talk to you, you go and find a trusted adult." He smiles to himself, proud of how well he remembered that.

"Exactly that Jim. And for now, this man is a stranger. He isn't a typical patient, so I need you to give him space for now and stick with the people you trust."

I watch as he tries to understand. "I'm going to put on another jumper," he finally announces before going off to his room.

He understands. If he didn't, he wouldn't have felt the need to put another jumper on for safety. That's his thing. We can all tell what kind of day Jim is having by how many jumpers he puts on. On his best day, he only wore two.

Tom prowls over, takes one glance through the window at the new guest and rolls his eyes. "Boring.

Could have been a nice bit of crumpet instead," he says before skulking off back to his room.

"Everything ok ladies?" Loretta breezes her way down the corridor towards us.

"I don't know, this is making my anxiety play up." Katie is the first to answer; if her skin wasn't so yellow I can imagine she'd be looking quite pale.

"Everything is under control. He will be on one-to-one for a little while and you know if there are any problems you just press the emergency button."

Katie nods but I don't think that has helped ease her anxiety at all.

"Anyway, I came to borrow Lisa. Lisa? Can you follow me into the office for a minute."

Lisa shrugs and follows Loretta back down the corridor, leaving me and Katie nervously standing by the lounge window, wondering if we should be locking ourselves away in our rooms instead.

Jim appears just as the new guy joins us in the corridor with two of the healthcare assistants. The first thing he does when he sees Jim is stand up straight, shoulders back, before bringing his face close to his and squaring up to him. Then he jolts his head forward in that horrible football hooligan way, like he's trying to startle him.

Absolute wanker.

One of the assistants takes him by the arm and leads him away.

"This way Antony, let's show you to your room now."

Antony, so that's his name. I can't stand Antony.

He turns back to stare out Jim with a sly, unkind smirk.

"What the fuck you got five jumpers on for anyway, you fucking retard?" he growls as he's dragged away, followed by a loud laugh, like this is pure entertainment for him.

Poor Jim has gone red in the face, unsure what to say or how to feel. I can see blotches appearing on his neck, like stress hives. I'm not sure whether this is about to throw him into a meltdown or not.

"I'm going to find Loretta now because she's my trusted adult," he mumbles, his voice shaky.

"Oh, she's with Lisa at the moment…"

"Then I'll WAIT OUTSIDE!" he shouts, startling me and Katie. I've never heard him shout, but it's not out of anger but rather fear and confusion. I notice just before he turns on his heel that his eyes are filled with tears.

As he walks towards Loretta's office, he punches himself in the head twice. I can hear him muttering the disgusting word Antony called him.

Suddenly I don't want to be here anymore. I have never felt trapped before, but right now I feel like I could be caged in with a dangerous animal.

CHAPTER THIRTEEN

WALKING STICK FOR THE WALKING PRICK

Late that afternoon, the second patient arrives: female, eighteen, from London and looking like she might punch me in the face if I look at her wrong. The vibe in this place has definitely now taken an uncomfortable shift.

Sure, all of us have our own individual problems but none of us have been afraid that we could be attacked by another – until now.

Her name is Stacey and she's only been in her room for about an hour when she walks into mine and helps herself to my books and chocolate and takes them back to her own room. I'm not around when she does it, but people see her. I am just about to knock on her door and ask her to give my stuff back when I hear giggling. I peak through the window to see her and Antony laughing together on her bed. Oh God, she's already made friends with Damian. This could be really bad news for the rest of us.

By dinner time, the two are inseparable. As we go down to the dining room, they mostly ignore everyone else around them and behave like they are in their own little bubble – though to be fair, it is probably better this way. At least Antony is leaving Jim and everybody else alone. Jim has six jumpers on tonight – six! I guess the thought of having dinner with this dickhead didn't exactly thrill him either.

I was hating every moment of this. During dinner, Antony purposely spills his soup on the floor and he and Stacey laugh in a horrible mocking way whilst the cook cleans it up. And then, whilst Jim is buttering his roll, Antony leans over and spits on it. I gag. It is gross – but worst of all is how much of a kick he is getting out of upsetting us all. He is disgusting, the worst human being I have ever met and if I wasn't so concerned that he would smash his walking stick over my head, I'd have picked up Jim's roll and thrown it at Antony's fucking peanut head.

We barely speak a word during dinner. Lisa watches him and Stacey the whole time, sizing them up, trying to understand them I presume. Katie keeps her eyes on her meal at all times and so does Jim.

Inside, I am like a volcano bubbling away: how dare somebody so new just turn up and completely change how comfortable and safe we feel in our temporary home? Katie is so anxious she tried to kill herself last week. People here do not cope well with stress and here he is, a mountain of fucking stress, upsetting everybody.

The second we are all back on the ward, things get worse. Antony lies on one sofa, his legs up so nobody else can sit, and throws his walking stick onto the opposite sofa so no one can sit there either. Stacey is sitting on one of the tables with each of her feet resting on two chairs, smirking as if she's just dying for somebody to challenge her.

The rest of us walk past them and head out into the conservatory instead. Jim has some regular cards with him and he asks me, Lisa and Katie to play snap with him, which we do. Tom goes off to his room. He tells us he needs a wank because of all the tension.

"Oi!" Stacey suddenly bellows from the living room and towards our direction. "How do you lot get hold of weed in this place?"

"We don't," Lisa answers, matter-of-factly.

"That's bollocks, there's always drugs in places like this."

Now Antony sits up and leans forward in our direction. "If any of you lot have anything in your rooms, go get it now, I want it."

"We don't," Lisa answers for us again, firm and confident.

It suddenly occurs to me that Antony is supposed to be on one-to-one, so is Katie come to think of it, but it's only us lot here.

"How am I supposed to believe there's no drugs in

here when that bitch is yellow?" He's pointing at Katie. "So there must be at least some pills in his place."

"There isn't. I got into the medicine cupboard last week and grabbed some Lorazepam."

"Nice!" He laughs, all impressed for the first time.

"Not really, she almost died," I surprise myself by saying.

"Oh well, shit happens. Go to the cupboard now and get me and Stace some."

"I can't…" Katie mumbles. "It's locked."

"So how the fuck did you manage it before?"

"The dispenser guy left the door unlocked by accident. When I noticed that, I just took my opportunity. They're being extra cautious since that though; there's no chance they'll make the same mistake again."

"Well, you best try, because I need something."

"Aw, well, she can't. She's not your lackey," Lisa intervenes.

"Who are you to keep piping up? You fat dyke!"

Lisa just laughs. "When there are men like you, no wonder I'm a *dyke.*"

Just as Antony rises to his feet to challenge her, one of the healthcare assistants walks in. Finally, Antony is back on one-to-one, and the presence of a staff member seems to break up the tension. Antony sits back on the sofa, but not before winking at Lisa like he wants her to know she is going to pay for talking back.

CHAPTER FOURTEEN
ARTS, CRAFTS & DEATH THREATS

The vibe the next morning is so much better, mainly because Antony and Stacey aren't down at Art therapy with us. Stacey has her first therapy session with Maddie and Antony has a meeting with some posh-looking men and Dr Pope, who I am hoping will be discussing whether Antony should even stay here. I hope with everything I have that they choose to move him somewhere else. Anywhere. Baghdad might be nice.

Our art teacher I guess you could call her is a total vibe – she wears dungarees and always has a brightly coloured scarf in her hair; she has the most laid-back attitude, she's always happy and smiling, but most of all she plays the best music. Today she's brought with her a club classics album and whilst we all get stuck into painting, she blasts some Fedde le Grand – "Put Your Hands Up for Detroit" – for us all.

The atmosphere is *so* calming compared to yesterday

and I'm grateful for the relief. Everyone is in conversation, discussing hobbies and things that they did before they became unwell or ended up in hospital. I'm quite surprised when Katie tells me she used to practise guitar a lot at home; I hadn't pegged her for a musician but now she says it, I suppose she does have a little bit of a rock n roll, emo kind of edge.

"Mine's football. I used to play for the ladies' team where I live. Midfield," Lisa adds.

Tom laughs. "Wow, a dyke that likes football. Shocking."

Lisa just sticks her middle finger up at him but she's not the least bit offended.

"At least I just play for a local team and don't believe I actually own Portsmouth FC."

I can't help but burst out laughing at that one.

"Lisa!" our art teacher warns.

"I *do* own Portsmouth! How else do you explain my Aston Martin? Or my Porsche 911? Or my Range Rover with the heated seats and tinted windows for when I don't want to be recognised? How would I afford all that if I wasn't a football manager?"

Obviously, none of us have seen these cars. I don't even think he has a driving licence.

The corner of Lisa's mouth tips up, I can tell she's concealing a laugh. There's so much she could say, but she doesn't. It's a tough one with Tom – he dishes out a lot of insults but there's not much you can say back because it can mess with his mind.

"You're right, Tom," she says instead. "I forget you actually own the club, my bad."

Tom stares blankly for a moment, unsure whether she's being sincere but soon nods. "Ok, thank you. I'll sort you out some free tickets when we are out of here if you want. Box ones."

"That'll be nice, cheers. Don't forget to introduce Chloe to Channing Tatum as well, remember?"

"What?"

Now I'm trying not to laugh because the poor guy looks completely confused. I guess when you tell a lot of lies you struggle to remember them all.

"Oh yeah," he grunts. "He's gone back to the States for the moment, but I will when he comes back."

"Thanks Tom, that'll be nice." I smile.

The conversation continues this way for another half an hour or so, just us gathered around a table, painting, discussing things we enjoy doing outside of this place and having a laugh in the process. That is, until the door swings open and in walks a healthcare assistant chauffeuring none other than Stacey and Antony.

"Oh great, the Lidl version of Bonnie and Clyde are back," Tom groans.

The art teacher attempts to take control. She offers Antony and Stacey a place to sit and shows them all the different things they can do, whether it's painting, colouring or sculpting. They both turn their noses up at everything she offers though, typically. Eventually, they do sit down but begin sniggering and whispering between themselves and staring at us individually. It's giving off playground behaviour vibes, but I remind myself I am here to better myself, not worry about what two people like them think of me.

"There's a ping pong table outside," Antony states, looking out of the patio doors.

"Would you like to do that instead?"

He nods and his one-to-one assistant agrees it's ok, so off they go, he and Stacey, outside and out of our hair.

I soon finish the water colour painting I've been doing; it's not great, I'm no artist, but I actually quite like it. Our art teacher encourages us to paint memories that made us happy or pictures of somewhere we'd like to be one day as a manifestation technique.

So I drew a sun setting on a beach in Florida, no particular one in mind, and in the distance are dolphins in the water and birds flying through the sky. An American flag stands tall in the sand dunes. It represents a memory and a hope for the future. When I was younger, around twelve years old, my dad had planned to take me and my sister to Disney World; my mum wasn't coming with us because she had a terrible fear of flying. We were so excited anyway that we got to go with Dad. He worked around the clock, so the opportunity of quality time with him was a huge plus. But then a few months before we were due to go, he had a heart attack and ended up in hospital for a while. I remember being so scared, not about the holiday, I couldn't care less about Florida at that point, but about losing him.

Thankfully, not only did he bounce back, but he was adamant he still wanted to take us to Florida – a bold move considering his doctor said under no circumstances was he to put himself in a stressful situation. I definitely think a long-haul flight with two children counts as stress! But he did it anyway, he didn't want to let us down and I think he wanted to make those memories for us all. So we went, and it was amazing. And one day, I'll be back there. If my dad can overcome a heart attack and go, then I can beat this and go. One day.

"Nice work Chlo," the art teacher comments. "Why don't you pop it on the bench outside, it'll dry quicker under the sun."

I head outside, ignoring Antony and Stacey who are mid game at the ping pong table.

I'm placing my painting down on the bench when I suddenly feel the hairs on the back of my neck stand up. I realise in that moment that Antony is standing right behind me, peering over my shoulder.

"Aw, that's cute, do you get a sticker for completing that?"

I can't help it, but I do feel a bit embarrassed. I know some people will probably think it's childish, to be sitting around and making pictures like we're in nursery, but the fact is that it's a good distraction, it's one of my favourite things to do here.

I roll my eyes and walk away, but I'm barely back inside when I hear the sound of paper ripping. Sure enough, I turn around to see Antony tearing my painting to shreds whilst Stacey laughs her head off. I don't know what he expected to happen here – I'm not three years old, I'm not going to cry. It is what it is. So I just shrug my shoulders and walk off.

"Hey Chloe…" he calls after me. I didn't even realise he knew my name.

I reluctantly turn around and my eyes meet his.

"The second I find you on your own without staff to rely on, I'm going to shove this bat so far up your pussy I'll be rupturing your insides and laughing whilst you bleed out."

His finger is pointing not to his ping pong bat but to the cricket bat in the sports box on the floor. He grins, baring all his dark yellow teeth, and his eyes are dark and cold. I glance at Stacey, thinking that as a woman maybe she'll think that he has gone too far, but her eyes narrow onto mine and she looks eerily comfortable with the idea.

I don't know how I just became his target, I didn't even really realise I was on his radar, but I am and now I feel sick.

***

"Please Loretta," I plead when I'm back from Art therapy. "Please tell Dr Pope that this is really urgent. I want to go home."

She sighs, one hand on her hip. "What's brought all this on? You've been doing fine here."

"Nothing. I just want to go *home. PLEASE* Loretta." My voice is growing more and more desperate.

"Chloe, you're here because you need to be. We can't just let you go; a whole team of people have to agree when it's time for you to be discharged and unfortunately that hasn't happened yet."

Tears sting my eyes as I try to swallow the thick lump that's formed in my throat.

"You've got an hour until dinner, why don't you go to your room and relax for a little while? Come and find me later if you're still feeling this low."

I could stamp my feet and throw a tantrum in this place, and I know full well I'm not getting out of those doors that easily.

I walk quickly to my room, hoping that I can hold the tears back until I get there, but the second I step inside, I find Antony sitting on my bed, reading through my journal.

He stares up with that horrible look on his face and grins.

"I have a fun plan for tonight. You in?"

CHAPTER FIFTEEN

THE UN-GREAT ESCAPE

I have to get out of here. I can't do what Antony wants me to do, it's evil. But he says if I don't, what he'll do to me will be much worse. He says if I even think about grassing on him and telling the staff, then it'll be even worse for me. And it's not like I can avoid him – we both live here for now. His room is just a few doors up from mine. I don't have much faith the staff can keep me safe at all times, because even though they do their best, things do happen. Katie got pills in here. Tom ruined my bed sheets in here. Things *do* happen. All he'd have to do was creep into my room one night and nobody would know.

"How do you escape?"

"What?" Lisa looks at me suspiciously and probably in surprise since I just burst into her room and didn't even knock.

"Like hypothetically? How would a person escape?

The doors are locked, so how? I did think about shimmying out the window with a rope made out of bed sheets but that sounds like a disaster waiting to happen…"

"And the windows are sealed."

"And that. So how Lisa? How did you escape?"

"It's easier than you think. When the staff take us out for walks to like Knole Park, I usually run away then. Only once did I escape from the ward but that was only because the door hadn't closed itself properly behind a staff member. But it's like a one in a million chance that'll ever happen again."

We only have like half an hour until it's time to go down for dinner, so a walk won't be happening. That's usually a lunchtime thing.

"Why don't you ask to be taken for a walk around the gardens? They may allow that."

My mind races with the thought. The whole building is surrounded with greenery and flowers. They're really nice grounds to walk around. The front garden has a fountain and patches of grass with beds of flowers on them. Then there's gravel and the car park and *then* there's the exit. If I run, I could make it out. Eventually, you come to a village I think, but then I'm sure I could cut through Knole Park, that way I could probably make it to the train station within about fifteen or twenty minutes if I walked fast.

I loiter around the staffroom window, trying to look calm. If I want someone to take me outside for some fresh air and a walk, I need to not look suspicious.

Suddenly, the window slides open and a young, slim girl with long blonde hair smiles at me brightly. "Hello! Chloe, isn't it?"

"Er, yes."

She looks happy to see me which is strange because I don't recognise her at all.

"I'm Becky, I usually work upstairs but I'm with you guys tonight covering a shift. I heard you listening to garage music earlier, so I had to ask the ladies who you are and they said *Chloe!* Loving the taste in music Chloe!"

Wow, she's like if sunshine were an actual person. She's very pretty, her smile is bright and infectious with the most perfect white teeth I've ever seen.

"Oh yeah…" I answer, a little thrown off. "I love garage music."

She nods enthusiastically in agreement. "So, what can I do you for?"

Ok, stick to the plan, Chlo. You want to go for a walk. Then you're going to make a run for it.

"I just wondered if Loretta was around. I was feeling a little cabin fever-ish and was really hoping we could maybe go for a little walk around the grounds."

"Ah! Well Loretta is busy getting things prepared for handover tonight, but if I go and check with her, I'm sure I can take you outside for ten minutes."

Oh for fuck's sake. I wanted Loretta. She's fifty years old, a little frumpy, asthmatic, she's the only one I could potentially outrun. If I've got to go up against sports Barbie, then I've got no chance. This is like when I was eight years old and used to think I could beat Jet from *Gladiators* in the Eliminator. In fact, I've probably got more chance of that. This girl looks seriously athletic.

"Oh, that's ok, I'll wait for Loretta."

"Oh…" She peers over her shoulder at Loretta who looks to be having a serious conversation on the phone and then back to me. "I really don't think it'll be possible."

Ok, a small chance is better than no chance, right? Maybe she isn't as athletic as she looks. Maybe she has a bad ankle. Maybe she's a really heavy smoker and after running ten feet she'll have a coughing fit and then I can make my great escape. I could bunk a train, maybe go to a mate's house, they might put me up in secret if I tell them the story. Eventually, I'll have to let Dad know that I'm safe but hopefully by then, Antony will have moved on.

"Ok then, yes please. If you don't mind?"

"Of course not!" Her face lights up. "Let me just let Loretta know when she's got a second and then I'll come grab you from your room."

When I get back to my room, I'm like Mr Motivator on *GMTV*. I'm doing lunges, squats, calve stretches, everything I can think of to get myself in the best shape of my life within five minutes. I try to ignore the fact that on my fifth squat I fart and startle myself. I can't lose focus. I *need* to get out of here.

"Ready, Chloe?" She appears in my doorway, one arm already in a light jacket and I'm convinced for a second that I notice her lip curl up in disgust and I'm pretty sure that means she just caught a whiff of my anxious bowels, but she composes herself quickly.

It's a beautiful late spring evening when we get outside. The sun is slowly setting but the air is still warm and humid. The birds are gently singing, high up in the trees, and there's very minimal breeze. It would be a really enjoyable walk, if I wasn't gearing myself up to leg it.

"Ooh, it's lovely out here isn't it?"

"Yeah."

"D'you know, I went to see DJ Luck and MC Neat once in London, they were so good. I think they're doing a few more venues soon, you should go."

"Yeah." Sorry, but I can't engage in conversation right now hun, I'm busy eyeing my exit. I see it perfectly. Right at the end of the gravel driveway there's the exit. No gates, nothing, just a space between two brick walls big enough to fit a car through. I just need to get there. Then I need to go right. Or maybe it's left…

"Oh wow! Look at that sunflower!" Becky points behind us. "It's nearly as big as me."

And that's the moment – whilst Becky is looking away from me, I seize the opportunity and run.

Now, the only way I can describe the next thirty seconds of my life is pathetic. I ran, farted and ran some more.

It reminds me of that scene in *Identity Thief* where Melissa McCarthy tries running away from Jason Bateman and whilst Melissa is sprinting as fast as she can, Jason is merely doing a slow jog and easily keeps up with her.

That was me. I barely made it to the end of the driveway before sports Barbie overtook me with ease, while I was practically hyperventilating with a sheen of sweat above my lip. Embarrassing really when I had only run about eighty feet. I'm also fairly certain she didn't even start chasing me straight away – it's like she felt sorry for how slow I was and gave me a pitiful head start.

Either way, she's now standing in front of me, a flash of disappointment passing across her face, using her walkie talkie to talk in code to security back in the hospital. She knows I'm not going to try and run again; I'm far too out of breath. I wonder what code fourteen means anyway. If I had to guess, it's something like *mentally ill obese bird just tried to run and it was lowkey hilarious, but can someone come and help me escort her back inside?*

Anyway, with my dignity in tatters, I return to the ward. Loretta shakes her head as soon as she clocks eyes on me. I have achieved nothing but embarrassment. Thank God nobody else saw me.

"Chloe!" Jim high fives me just before I pass his room in the hallway. "You run funny."

"What?"

"Just a minute ago, I saw you running out the window. You run a bit weird. And also, your head kind of bobs up and down as you run. Were you trying to escape? Because I think your first mistake was that you probably didn't run fast enough."

"Yes. I know that, Jim. And no, I wasn't *escaping,*

there was a wasp. It was following me; I had to run away from it."

"Oh, that's alright then." He seemingly buys my terrible lie. I slink off to my room. I have no more ideas. That was it, that was my best plan to get away from Antony, at least for now, and it backfired. Fuck.

CHAPTER SIXTEEN

I'M SORRY, JIM

There's a new person Antony jokes with on the walk down to the dining room tonight, and it's me.

Since his little chat with me in my bedroom, it seems I'm getting the free pass he promised. He treats me more like he treats Stacey. I almost feel like I've been recruited into his 'gang' and that means I'm now safe from being his enemy.

Inside, I feel uncertain and scared. But on the surface, I act calm. I keep Antony laughing and joking with me because this side of him is much better than the guy who wanted to hurt me. I don't want to lose this fake friendship. If I'm to survive in here, I guess this is the type of person I need to be friends with.

Nobody really questions it either; if anything, it prompts Lisa and Katie to join in with our conversation at dinner. They probably think he has just mellowed out and is growing more settled here and that all the anger before was just a front. Jim picks up on the sudden improvement in atmosphere too and it excites him. He raises his glass of milk and tries to make a toast; he clinks all our glasses, spilling each one with his clumsiness.

"To friendship!" he beams, making everybody smile.

Antony catches my gaze and winks. I snap my gaze away and stare down at my glass of water instead. I'm so consumed with guilt already that I can't even look at poor Jim. He is so happy, but he has no idea what I'm about to do to him. What Antony wants me to do.

I finish my dinner quicker than everybody else so that I can be the first person excused from the table. I beg one of the assistants to walk me back to the ward, pretending that I've come on my period and need to grab pads.

They agree and thankfully this means I am the first and only patient on the ward. Since I'm not on a one-to-one, the assistant soon disappears off into the staffroom and I make my way down the corridor and towards the bedrooms. I don't have time to stall because the others will be back any minute and I have to get this done.

A quick scan behind me to make sure no staff members are watching me, then I quickly slip into Jim's room. It's spotless; he has four brightly coloured jumpers neatly folded on his desk, ready to be worn tomorrow. His blue and white striped pyjamas are also neatly folded on his pillow, ready for bed. It's so adorable and yet I have to ignore that completely, because I'm here for something else.

I check over his desk but there's nothing; his

backpack sits on the floor next to his wardrobe, so I rifle through that but nothing there either.

I gently slide open the drawer of the bedside table, careful not to make too much noise, and there they are – Jim's prized possession. His Pokémon cards.

I grab them and get out of his room as quickly as possible.

Back in the corridor, I'm still alone. I can't hear any of the voices of the other guys coming back from dinner yet, so I still have time.

***

"What shall we do tonight? Watch a movie?" Katie asks.

"You *always* want to watch a movie," Lisa laughs. "We should do something else, play cards again maybe."

The pair tap on my bedroom door. I'm sitting on the bed, having just got into my pyjamas, trying my best not to look as guilty as I feel.

"You wanna come hang out with us in the lounge?" Lisa asks.

I'm not sure if I do really. I'd rather hide away but that'll just look worse. I need to face the music to what I've done. I nod with a nervous smile and follow them out. I see that Jim has already gone into his room. He usually goes to collect his Pokémon cards after dinner – the only times they're not in his hands are when we are down in the dining room.

I catch a glimpse of a smug-looking Antony and I look away. I can't bring myself to look at him right now, but I can tell from the corner of my eye that he is still watching me. Revelling in what is about to happen. If he wants me to join him in laughing about this, he won't have any luck. My heart is racing out of my chest, and every beat is regret. I want to cry, I want to run away, but that would be a cowardly way out now.

We barely make it into the lounge when Jim comes rushing out of his room with pure panic in his voice.

"Has anyone seen my Pokémon cards?"

I look at the floor. It's starting.

"No? Did you take them down to dinner with you?" Katie asks.

"No! I'd never do that in case I spill something on them. I keep them in my safe place for breakfast, lunch and dinners but they're not there now."

His face is blotchy and red; I know that stress rash by now.

"Ok. We can help you look?" she offers.

"I've looked everywhere in my room. Please, if somebody has taken them for a joke, please give them back, *please.*"

His voice grows shakier with each word and a stutter that I didn't know he had until now is coming out. I'm now learning that Jim has a stutter when he gets anxious and it's all because of me.

He paces the hallway, squeezing his eyes tight every so often like he is desperately trying to magic the answer to pop into his brain.

Then the sobs start. He full-on starts crying like a small toddler who somehow got separated from his parents in the supermarket. He looks lost. He is completely freaking out.

"Jim, it's ok," Antony announces. "Someone in here took your Pokémon cards. Maybe if you ask really nicely, they'll give them back to you."

"Who? *Please* tell me who, please, I'll do anything." Jim's hands come up to his chest in a prayer sign.

He looks between us all, trying to work out who took them. His bottom lip is quivering, his eyes are wide and desperate but growing puffy and red.

"Well, they're not going to tell you like that, Jim! You need to get on your hands and knees and beg."

"No, no, Jim! Don't do that…" I interrupt but Jim is already on the floor, hands in the air, pleading as if he's fighting for his life.

"Now…" Antony continues with a vicious smile. "Kiss all of our feet."

"No, stop," I blurt out. "It was me Jim, I took them."

"Ooh, wow. Did you hear that everyone? Chloe, of all people. A real wolf in sheep's clothing." I hate Antony right now but nowhere near as much as I hate myself.

"Oh! Please Chloe, please can I have them back."

"You can't, no – because she tore them up into little pieces, didn't you? Chloe?" And with that, he bursts out laughing like he's finally revealed the punchline.

The scream that comes from Jim is soul shattering. He looks like he has just been told a loved one has died. Tears stream down his face, snot runs from his nose, his face is beetroot red, and he is breaking down in front of us all – because of me.

I drop down to his level and try my best to get him to focus on me, to hear me over his screaming.

"Jim, shh, listen Jim, I didn't rip them. I promise." I couldn't bring myself to do that. "But I did hide them."

"Where?" He leaps up to his feet, clinging on to that one seed of hope.

"Well, there's some in the microwave, some in the fridge…" Oh god, it's raining. I didn't know it was raining. "I threw some out of the window."

"But why? They're going to get wet and ruined… Loretta!" Jim begins to shout in a desperate panic. "Loretta please open the back door, QUICK!"

I now have to tell Loretta what I did, and her expression starts with confusion and ends in pure disappointment.

Her hands are frantic as she finds the right key, she knows only too well how much these cards mean to Jim.

By some grace of God, or probably more because there's a slight shelter over the window, the cards are found with minimal damage, but a few are still damp.

Nobody says anything, we just watch on as a shaken Jim wipes the damp cards down with a kitchen towel Loretta gives him.

"I don't understand," he eventually says, filling the silence and looking directly at me. "I thought we were friends."

***

After I've spent half an hour back in my room crying, I know I need to speak to Jim, I need to somehow make him feel a little better or at the very least I need him to know that he didn't deserve that.

I tap lightly on his door and see him sitting cross-legged on his bed with his Pokémon cards laid out in front of him.

"Can I come in?"

"Of course!" He looks up at me with a small sincere smile. "You look like you've been crying. What's wrong? Do you need a hug?"

The fact he is offering me a hug after what I did just shows the magnitude of his innocence and it takes everything to hold back the tears once more. I just wanted to feel safe again in here and I hurt Jim in the process, which in turn has hurt me. I'll never ever get that image of what I did to him out of my head, ever.

I mumble something about being ok and I sit on his chair at the desk.

"Are they all ok?" I gesture towards the cards.

"Yes. I've counted them five times and they're all here and the damp ones are nearly dry now, so it's ok. Thank you for telling me where they were, it was a good prank, I'm sorry I ruined it."

He's killing me.

"No Jim, it wasn't a prank. It was nasty and I need you to understand how sorry I am, because I *am* your friend, at least I hope I am, and that is *not* how a friend treats another friend."

"Then why did you do it?"

Because Antony threatened to sexually assault me with a cricket bat. Because Antony said if I didn't do this, he'd beat me with his walking stick until I left this place unrecognisable. And because I'm a fucking coward.

"I made a choice, but it was the wrong choice. There's no reason good enough to do that to somebody Jim and I'm just so sorry…"

His warm hand comes up to my back to comfort me. "No, it's not ok, Jim. I want you to understand that if anybody ever does that to you again, or anything else that causes you pain like that, you stay away from them because they're *not* your friend and they don't deserve you or your kindness, ok? You don't ever deserve to be treated like that."

"Ok. Except you though, right?"

I make a *harumph* sound. "I don't know right now."

"Well, I think I do. I think you're a good person who made a bad decision and that's ok. Because I forgive you."

His blue eyes, still red from crying, stare straight into mine. I can see in his eyes that he believes what he just said.

But I'm unconvinced. I go to bed and cry myself to sleep that night, replaying the moment I broke somebody who saw me as a *friend.*

CHAPTER SEVENTEEN
BREAKING POINT

So, I wake up with a clear plan in mind. Avoid Antony like the plague and follow Jim round like a lost puppy, offering to do anything and everything. Make his bed? No problem. Fold his five jumpers for tomorrow? Easy. Spit-shine his shoes? Weird, but I'd do it. At this point, there isn't much I won't do to fix yesterday and be the better friend that Jim deserves.

"We need to talk." Lisa almost bumps into me as I'm leaving my room. She ushers me back inside, with a serious expression on her face. This feels awkward straight away.

"What the hell was that about yesterday? If Antony was putting you up to something like that, you should have come and spoken to me first, I'd have sorted it."

I think at some point during the many years that Lisa has been in and out of this place, she appointed herself as some kind of unofficial top dog. She thinks she is entitled to know everything about everyone and to be told about any problems she might be able to solve. In her mind, because she has spent so much time here and this really has been like a home, she feels responsible.

I want to ask her what she expects to be able to do against a man? But I don't want to make her feel inferior, I know she takes her role here seriously.

"I didn't want anyone else to have to fight my battles," I say instead. "We don't know him, we have no idea what he is truly capable of. I thought, stupidly, that I was making the best choice last night. I was never going to rip them up, but I thought what I did was enough, and that Antony would leave me alone and that Jim would be a bit pissed off but nothing terrible and that would be that."

She rolls her eyes in response. "Well first of all, you're an idiot. Once Antony got you to do one thing, he was only going to come up with more shit that he'll make you do for him. It wouldn't have stopped at Jim."

Sigh. She's right.

"And as for Jim…"

"Oh no, Lisa, please don't. I can't bear to hear any more of what I've done to him. I feel awful. I'm worse than Saddam Hussein, like if Saddam Hussein and Rose West had a lovechild, it would probably be me at this point."

"I don't know who Rose West is?" She stares at me blankly.

"It's not important."

"I actually wasn't going to say anything bad; I was

going to say that Jim is ok this morning, he's his usual cheery self and he only has three jumpers on."

Three jumpers *is* a good sign.

But even if Jim has forgotten all about it, I certainly haven't. I'm not sure if I ever will.

"You just need to accept that you fucked up and move on."

I shrug, I don't really know what to say, I don't feel like I deserve to move on.

"You are sorry, aren't you?"

My eyes snap up to meet hers. "Yes of course I am! I regret it more than anything, you know I care for Jim, I'm so angry at myself it's unbelievable."

"Well, there you go. You're sorry, you regret it. We live and learn, so put it down as a lesson and move on."

"But I still have Antony to worry about."

"Don't. I solved that, I told Loretta all about him last night."

Oh my god. He's definitely going to hit me with that bloody walking stick now.

"Lisa? Why!? He's gonna go mad…"

"It'll be fine, I'm here."

Oh for fuck's sake. She's doing it again, thinking she's the Rocky Balboa of this place. I like Lisa a lot and I trust she always has good intentions but there's just no way she's going to win against a boy like him and I worry that she just put me in a dangerous position.

***

I'm comfortable enough to chill in the lounge area for a

while since I know Antony is in his therapy session with Maddie.

I've spent the last hour watching Jim rank all his Pokémon cards from his most to least favourite. It's mind-numbingly boring but I remind myself that I deserve this punishment. I'd put myself through fifty hours of it if I had to. I'd probably die of boredom, but it is what it is.

Tom's in the corner of the room flicking through an *Autotrader* magazine, circling possible new cars he wants to buy next week. Lisa and Katie are sitting opposite me on the sofa watching *Friends* on the TV.

I'm surprised when I see Stacey walking in to join us, she usually stays in her room if Antony isn't around.

She looks more pissed off than usual, her complexion is a little pale but the glare in her eyes is dark as always.

"You wait until Antony is back from therapy," she warns me. "You really crossed a line."

I genuinely have no clue what she's talking about.

"What?"

"Telling on him, pah! I knew you were pathetic but being a grass? That's new."

"I haven't told on anyone; I just want to be left alone."

"Well, you've done quite the opposite. He is raging mad. Because of you, they've had to phone his uncle and tell him about the threats and that's crossed a line."

She says it like he is terrified of his uncle and like I'm now supposed to feel bad for that, but I had no clue.

I don't know anything about Antony or why he is here, all I know is that he has a huge anger problem and threatens everyone.

I look at Lisa and she looks at me, guilt in her eyes.

"I grassed him up. If that's what he is so angry about then he should be angry with me," she informs Stacey.

"Nah, nice try but if Chloe wasn't such a pussy about these Pokémon cards and hadn't made a huge fuss about it, crying and everything, you wouldn't have known. She did it on purpose. Silly little attention seeker."

Lisa looks like she's about to protest some more but before a word can come out, Antony turns the corner. He instantly stares at me, his sly smirk back on his face.

Heather is trailing behind; she's obviously his one-to-one today.

"Anything to say Chloe?" he spits.

Yeah. How was therapy? Any chance they managed to fix your aggression in that one session? I look him up and down, it sure doesn't look like it. He is gripping the handle of his walking stick so hard his knuckles have gone white. This is it, I think, at any moment he is going to attack me with it.

"I-I did w-what you asked?" I try to sound calm and unaffected but I'm stuttering.

He laughs. "You put his cards in the fucking microwave! What was that supposed to do?"

"Enough Antony or you'll have to spend the rest of the day in your room," Heather warns.

And then it all happens so quickly. Antony raises his walking stick and the first thing he does is smash all the cups off the coffee table. It startles us all. Jim stands up to try and protect us girls, but Antony shoves the end of the stick right between Jim's legs, sending him straight down to the floor, cupping his balls, crippled in pain. I heard that hurts.

Heather runs over to the emergency button and presses it. All staff members are trained to be here within thirty seconds when that alarm sounds, but thirty seconds may be too long. How many times can somebody hit you in thirty seconds? Twice? Three times? Will I even be conscious by the time they get here?

Antony revels in the drama. He waves his stick high in the air and laughs loudly, like a psychopath actually.

"This stick is going up your cunt and is going to rip your organs out."

"You'll have to get through me first." Heather's now in front of me, shoulders back, head high, looking Antony square in his face, letting him know that she means business. She isn't going to stand by and let him bully any of her patients.

In an attempt to startle her, he smashes his stick against the wall right next to her head, knocking the clock off. She holds her own though, not allowing him to affect her.

It seems to throw him off, having this face-off with her. I think he expected us to be running and cowering right now and maybe that's how he gets off. Terrifying women. But Heather is adamant she's not going to give him what he wants, no matter how intimidating he might be.

"Just whack her one!" Stacey shouts, but it's too late – half a dozen members of staff are now appearing in the room, including Jake the huge rugby guy. Within seconds, Antony has been restrained with ease, his walking stick removed from him and he is being manhandled out of the room. He doesn't even try to fight back against them; it's quite pathetic really, once you realise that he's scared himself. He's just a messed-up boy who wanted to scare some girls. Maybe it made him feel braver or bigger, but now, he just looks like a little boy with a bad attitude.

Thankfully, that was the last time I ever saw Antony; he was moved to a different hospital closer to London where I think they are better prepared to deal with people who might want to hurt others.

Jim manages to get to his feet now that all the commotion is over.

"Corr! My balls hurt!"

"Jim! Thank you so much for trying to help us, that was so sweet."

"Yes, very brave of you Jim, well done," Heather adds.

Slowly, our heads all turn to Tom who is just sat staring at us, his jaw slightly open, his eyes half rolled back like he is about ready to fall asleep. I would say it's down to medication, but Tom is strangely so laid back he can barely stand.

"What?" he grunts.

"Didn't fancy jumping in to help at any time Tom?" Lisa jokes.

He rolls his eyes. "Can't, wouldn't be a fair fight. I have a black belt, and I used to be a cage fighter. I'm trained to kill someone with one punch. So, not really allowed to get involved with amateurs."

Jim gives him a thumbs up. "Ah fair enough Thomas! You did the right thing."

"Sorry," I can't help but laugh. "What's the black belt in? Talking absolute shit?"

"Nah. For real." He continues his waffle. "I was once kicked out of karate class because I was physically so good and so strong they couldn't find anyone to fight me. They had to look international, but no one wanted to. There was this one kid in Germany, but he backed out when he saw a photo of me. Then there was this army man in America somewhere, but…"

At some point that afternoon, Tom stops listing countries where people were too scared to fight him, but I couldn't tell you when.

CHAPTER EIGHTEEN
YOU CAN'T FIX EVERYONE.

One of the hardest things that I have had to learn in life is that *we* as humans physically can't fix everybody, especially when we need fixing ourselves. But a good chunk of us are 'fixers'. We try to see the solutions and answers for people who show signs of struggle, and we try to make them better, make their life better. Often at the cost of our own wants and needs.

I have done this a lot throughout my life. I have stayed in terrible relationships and toxic friendships that didn't serve me at all but I wanted to help. My best example would be when I spent three years in a relationship with a functioning alcoholic. Being his partner came at a huge cost. One day, when my partner was drunk and had ruined another Christmas, I wondered if there would ever be a time we could enjoy something in life without it being ruined. Could we go on holiday and enjoy some time in the sun like normal people? I knew the answer was no, because several months earlier we went away for the weekend to York and he was drunk before we even checked-in and he remained drunk the entire time. We spent the majority of that weekend apart – he was out on his own, chasing that buzz, sitting in various pubs, making friends with people who he wouldn't remember the next day. And I hung out with the sixty-three-year-old hotel receptionist who took pity on me being on my own and started giving me jobs to do. *Jobs.* I was supposed to be on a romantic weekend away and instead I was doing fucking turn-down service for Hilton Hotels.

It was ridiculous but this was the life I was choosing for myself because no matter what I did for my partner to *fix* him, he wasn't ready to take the help. And the price was my happiness.

I wasted time setting up AA meetings, accompanying him to GP appointments, carrying the financial load when he got fired from another job due to an obscene number of absences because he was too hungover to work. He asked for my help many times, begged for it even, but every single time, when the time came, I was the only one ready to fight.

I wholeheartedly believed I could fix all the issues that led to his drink problem. From a bad childhood to low self-esteem, I was trying to put a plaster over all of it. Rather than just supporting him, I'd become responsible for him and that was and is the difference I understand in life.

I think the first person I ever tried to fix was Lisa.

I learned at some point after Antony had gone that Lisa's meeting with Loretta was in fact sad news. Lisa's mum had decided to up and move to Dublin for a new boyfriend which now meant that Lisa didn't have a home to go back to when she was discharged – she was now homeless.

I couldn't get the thought out of my head, how someone could just up and leave their unwell child. But most of all, all I could think about was how *I* could *fix* it. There had to be a way, there had to be something I could do.

Without realising it, I made Lisa's problem my problem and I couldn't relax until I found the solution.

Unfortunately, the solution came at the cost of my own wellbeing.

CHAPTER NINETEEN
WE COULD BE LIKE THE WALTONS… THE MENTALLY ILL VERSION.

Like all good plans, it began with utter delusion. I had already decided that we'd need to move in with my mum as she had a three-bedroom house and therefore had two spare and empty bedrooms. I know, moving back in with my mum would likely go down as well as asking Jimmy Saville to carry out my smear test. But I didn't have a choice – Lisa needed somewhere to live and a life to look forward to. It had only taken about ten minutes in my head, but I had it all worked out. Lisa and I would get jobs, we'd obviously contribute to my mum's mortgage and bills, we'd also save up on the side for our own flat which we'd eventually move into and then we'd start booking girls' holidays to places like Benidorm and Ibiza. It was absolutely foolproof. Three mentally unwell people under one roof – what could go wrong?

So that was the plan that I was set on. I could fix Lisa's homelessness and all I had to sacrifice was my own sanity by moving back in with my mum. Who was drinking less by all accounts but was still angry, unpredictable and not at all looking after herself.

By not looking after herself I mean both mentally and physically. She still wasn't sleeping properly, she'd wallow all night and sleep all day. My sister told me that in her fridge she had a tub of Flora and a pint of milk and on the side, some teabags and that was it. Oh, and a tin of shortbread from Christmas 1993. That was it. My mum wasn't eating which meant, as a type 1 diabetic, she was having a lot of hypos which she'd end up calling an ambulance for. She didn't have an oven or a toaster or any of the other basics that would make living with her any easier. She barely even bought herself toilet roll. She was in her own state of rock bottom and so really, even asking her to have two mentally unwell teenagers move in with her was pretty inconsiderate.

But I'm a fixer. I didn't concentrate on the millions of reasons why this was a bad idea, I just focused on the one positive it gave. And that would be a home for Lisa.

Today would be Mum's second visit and I was extra nervous. Last time she was here it ended in me trashing my room and her being asked not to come back unless she was invited. How fucking awkward was this going to be? But anyway, Lisa and I could be released within the next month, and I had to have a plan, I had to help her.

I sat on my bed whilst my mum literally picked up where we left off the last time I'd seen her.

"The thing with your dad, Chlo, is that he doesn't have your best interests at heart. If he did, he'd realise we need to all meet up instead of avoiding me like the cowardly wanker he is."

An insult towards my dad is always like a knife to my stomach. That may sound like favouritism but it's not, not really. My dad was just a good dad, a really good dad who loved me unconditionally and always tried to help me; even if he didn't really understand what was happening, he always did everything he could, his support was always there. I can't comment on their marriage, I wasn't in it, not like that obviously, and so I don't know the ins and outs. I can only judge my dad on how he is as my dad and not on what type of husband he was to my mum. And vice versa. But Mum's attitude was always that if he was a shitty husband then he was a shitty dad, a shitty friend, a shitty person.

Today, however, I let that insult wash over me. I usually say something but today I'm keeping her in a good mood, if I can.

It takes everything not to lunge off my bed at her when I see her picking up another marker and attempting to write Dad *another* message, despite the hospital already telling her that she cannot use me or my bloody whiteboard to communicate with my dad. Of course, she doesn't listen.

I just sit on my bed, refusing to look up and read the new message, and I try to stay focused. I *can* live with my mum; if it means Lisa has somewhere to stay, then I can do it. We won't even be home that much, we'll work loads and be out, we'll only really go home to sleep which means we won't really have to be around my mum that much. We can *totally* make this work.

My CD player that's been on shuffle begins playing Beyoncé, "Ring the Alarm". If you don't know the song, it starts with a siren sound. A siren sound which stops Mum in her tracks; with the pen still in her hand, she spins round to stare at me, wide-eyed and confused.

"What's that sound?" she whisper-shouts.

I nod at the CD player. "It's Beyoncé?"

"Oh Christ." She lets out a huge sigh of relief. "I thought they'd all escaped and that was a warning bell."

Escaped where I wonder? They're all walking around freely like they were last time she was here. I'm sure my mum thinks half of the patients are in padded cells, making scarves out of pubes or something. When the reality is really quite dull – half of them are probably just chilling with a Sudoku book. This quest with Lisa isn't going to go well if she thinks we are all alarmed and feral.

"Mum, I was thinking, maybe I could move in with you?" I say. May as well just get this over with.

She immediately puts the pen down and looks at me with half excitement and half disbelief. I know she's wondering if this is really happening – could I really be choosing to move back in with her after all this time? I don't want anyone to feel like I am just using any given opportunity here to slate my mum, but I know the reason she looks so happy isn't because of me. I'm sure on some level, she will enjoy the company again, but I know mostly, she'll just be happy that I'm choosing to leave Dad's house.

"Of course, you've always got a home with me, you know that."

"Thanks Mum… There's just one other thing…"

To be fair, my mum didn't really deserve to be bribed like this. In my head, I told myself she'd love it, it would be company and we'd have a laugh. Maybe it could be the making of me and Mum. But in reality, I knew how strained we were together and that bringing Lisa into it just wouldn't be fair on anyone.

But hey, I'm seventeen and I'm fixing someone else. I'm not thinking all that logically.

"You know Lisa?"

Her face instantly drops.

"Her mum has made her homeless…"

"What? Why?" she asks with a hint of genuine concern.

"She met this man and decided to move away. Lisa has nobody, Mum, she's going to be all alone. Me and her could move in with you, get jobs and contribute to all the bills. We'd help clean obviously and it could be so good for all of us…"

Even being the one selling it, I don't think I'd buy it. Mum looks unconvinced, so I just keep going like word vomit, listing off all the positive and yet delusional things that I think might sway her.

"What does your dad think of all this?" she asks when I finally stop for air.

"Well, he doesn't know…"

Her eyebrow arches as if to say, I wonder why…

Dad would tell me that I was here to get myself better, not to take on anyone else's problems and he'd be right. Of course he would be. But right now, I can't think about what is right, I just need to sort this out so that I can go and find Lisa and tell her I have fixed it all.

"Mum, please, think about it. You have two rooms just sitting empty, and we can help out so much around the house and you'll love Lisa…"

"Well, when would this happen?" She looks like I might actually be winning her over.

"It could be within the next month and then you won't have us for too long anyway because we are going to get a flat, we've got it all planned out."

"I'll think about it…"

"But Mum…" I can't stop protesting Lisa's case. "All the while it takes you to think about it, Lisa is worrying that she's homeless. Please, please?"

"Fine, ok, but just for a couple of months. You can stay for as long as you like but I can't be responsible for somebody else too, so you and Lisa will need to find somewhere else to live fairly quick."

I practically leap off the bed with the biggest spring in my step. "Thanks Mum! I really do appreciate this, I mean it. I'm going to tell Lisa."

This was the biggest thing my mum had ever done for me, and I felt after all the upset there had been, and all the trust that I had lost for her, that maybe this really could be a good thing. This could be the making of us.

At some point during the five minutes that I was

giving Lisa the best news, my mum had snuck out of my room, left the hospital and gone home. But not before telling the staff about my plan and how unfair it was to her.

Obviously looking back, I know that the idea was silly for many reasons and that my mum also needed to do what was right for her. I just wish she hadn't let me tell Lisa the good news first.

CHAPTER TWENTY

SOME PLANS ARE NEVER MEANT TO BE MATERIALISE

If you've ever tried to 'fix' someone in your life, then you'll know how difficult it is to just stop. Lisa didn't want me to stop, not to begin with; she wanted to live with me, but everyone in the hospital was really against the idea of me and Lisa spending more time together. My dad tried to understand my reasons, but he was unimpressed that I'd taken such drastic steps to make it happen. I felt like I'd let people down and made myself look silly, but I really did just want to help. It took a while to understand how naïve that was.

"The thing is, you don't *know* Lisa. You know the version of Lisa you see inside this hospital, but you don't know what Lisa is like on the outside." I'm now in Maddie's small therapy room. She has her hands resting on her lap and she's leaning close into me, almost like she wants to reach out and comfort me but doesn't.

"But nobody else was helping her…" My voice is small and embarrassed.

"She will get help; I can assure you of that. Nobody is going to let her leave here and become homeless."

"But I just feel like everyone is treating me like I have tried to do something awful."

Maddie smiles sympathetically. "No one thinks that. But two teenage girls struggling together with their mental illnesses has the prospect to be a real recipe for disaster. You could both damage your recoveries. And like I said, you don't know why Lisa is always back here, you don't know how she behaves on the outside and you'll never be able to get better and take care of her at the same time. Some people in here are complex. They only seem like they could cope with life fine because you're seeing a different side to them – they're safe in here, they are away from temptations and difficult situations. Do you get what I'm saying, Chloe?"

I thought I did. I was seventeen and I had thought I knew it all, but basically, I knew fuck all. This hospital is a bubble, she's right about that. There is so much we don't really tell each other because when it comes to mental health, it is still so hard to share the truth. On paper, I came in with an anxiety and panic disorder, low self-esteem and depression. It didn't say, *Chloe occasionally wets the bed in her sleep through anxiety, Chloe sometimes prays before she falls asleep that she won't wake up again, Chloe can't leave the house unless her dad is with her, Chloe can't walk inside a shop or a supermarket because her mind tells her she will stop breathing.* I could go on, but it would be exhausting. Equally, I don't know about Lisa – I don't know what causes her to put so many scars on her body or why she keeps returning here, I don't know what has happened in her childhood. We are two unwell young girls trying to navigate this illness and move onto a better life. There is no way either of us is in any position to support the other to such a huge degree.

It feels like the hardest thing to pull away from someone even though you need to. I have to trust that Lisa will be ok – the hospital staff are professionals who will not see her out on the streets, alone. And I am here to get better, which I'll be neglecting if I don't start concentrating on myself.

CHAPTER TWENTY-ONE
REFLECTION

It's been a strange couple of weeks inside this hospital and it's made me feel quite deflated to say the least. The plan was always just to come here and hopefully get better, to keep myself to myself. But when you're in these four walls twenty-four-seven, it seems just as easy to get caught up in other things. I got caught up with Antony, thinking I could give myself an easier ride and instead I hurt somebody else. I tried to help Lisa and all I did was damage my relationship with my mum even further and give Lisa an empty promise.

I knew being in here would be hard at times, but it's harder in so many other ways that I never could have known.

On top of that, I'm very much feeling like I have come to a halt in my therapy. I feel like everybody always pushes for the answer of when my anxiety first started, they want me to pinpoint a really triggering time so they can be like *A-ha! I knew it!* But I'm not having any of those moments. I'm tired of going over and over my childhood as if I'm missing some very crucial piece of the puzzle. Therapists always think something powerful has to have happened in childhood. But it didn't. For the most part, we were happy enough – we were looked after, loved, we travelled on amazing holidays and we were safe. But I feel like my anxiety has always been there, lurking in the background. I was always the kid who worried way more than my friends. Sure, by the time I got to my teenage years, my mum was definitely pulling it to the surface, but it was always there, it was always going to show itself, eventually.

And now, in an hour's time, I have a meeting with my dad and Dr Pope, and he's going to decide what the next course of action will be. I've been in this unit now for almost two months and I don't really know if I've learned anything. Was I supposed to learn something? Or is their job simply to stop me having anxiety attacks and staying awake all night? I don't know, but I'm far from cured. Will I ever be?

"How do you feel about the meeting, Chlo?" Dad asks. We're having a little walk outside in the hospital garden before Dr Pipe calls us in for the meeting. It's the most beautiful summer's day – blue skies, sunny, probably twenty degrees. Perfect.

"Scared," I answer honestly.

"Well don't be. If he thinks it's time to come home, then great, we can continue supporting you at home. If he thinks you should stay longer, then that's fine too – what's another month? You've already done two."

"Isn't it expensive to be here though?"

"Yes. But I'll remortgage the house if I have to. That's not something for you to worry about."

Wow, who'd have thought mental illness could be so expensive?

Dad and I spend the next half an hour sitting on a bench and enjoying the sunshine; it's relaxing and actually, the beautiful weather is making me wonder if it is time for me to leave. I love summer, it's my favourite season. I could be happier out of here, possibly.

***

After Dr Pipe finishes lecturing me about how he doesn't feel I am concentrating enough on my own recovery, and making me feel even more stupid and embarrassed for trying to help Lisa, he finally points out the positives.

"Well, you're sleeping better, and I hear from the nurses that although it takes you a while to settle, you are finally getting to sleep at a better time."

I nod, it's true, I am. I hate that I still find it really difficult. It's like as soon as my head hits the pillow and my body is expected to relax, I just can't. My brain goes into overdrive and I feel anxious and breathless, occasionally getting heart palpitations. Usually, none of it goes away until I just give up on sleeping. But lately, I am falling asleep better than before. I'm certainly not stuck lying awake all hours anymore, so that's a huge step forward.

"You've had one day in particular where it's reported you felt suicidal. Why was that?"

"Have you met my mother?" I half joke. He nods and then scribbles something down on his notepad.

He reads something else from the report and his eyebrows pinch together into a frown.

"It says here you've been reluctant to take medication for the panic attacks? Or for the nights you struggle to sleep."

"They make me groggy. They make my whole body feel numb and like I have no control. I don't like that feeling."

It's true. One night, they gave me something to stop my panic attack and it was an awful feeling. I felt like every part of my body was numb and felt restless, it was a really weird feeling that just made me scared. I got up and went straight to the male nurse who was in charge of dishing out medications and told him how crappy his drug had made me feel. He had very little sympathy, he just shrugged and told me to go to bed and sleep it off. But that felt impossible with restless legs. I felt like I was incredibly drunk – not in a good way, but in a way that made me worry I could accidentally hurt myself or pass out.

Dr Pipe makes a face like I'm being difficult or a diva, I don't know. He scribbles something else down and then gives me a lecture about the importance of taking medication when it is offered, because it will help.

Frustratingly, I feel like some people just don't appreciate how frightening new medications are to someone like me. I freak out at a Gaviscon!

I once took a painkiller and then was stupid enough

to read the list of side effects. There was a one-in-a-million chance of that painkiller causing me to go blind. Best believe I was an anxious mess for the rest of the day, completely convinced that my vision was darkening and I was losing my sight. Oddly, I still sometimes think I'm going blind. That's PTSD from taking a painkiller.

I sat with my Grandad once and asked him about World War Two, something he didn't speak about much. My dad said he had severe PTSD from the war and so didn't discuss much of what he saw or experienced. And then there's me. Thinking I can relate because I had an Ibuprofen.

"You participate in most things Chloe, but not outdoor exercise. Why is that?"

Have you ever been the fat one at Sports Day hun? That shit stays with you.

"I'm not very good at sports…" I answer.

"You don't have to be, it's the participating that counts."

Hmm. Ok. When I was around seven or eight, my sister and I were both asked by our parents if we'd like to do after-school activities. We both said yes. My sister chose to take up tap dancing, which luckily enough was taught in a little hut right next door to our house. I asked Mum if I could take up ballet. She absolutely loved the idea of me in a pink tutu, being all cute and chubby like a big round pink marshmallow. She practically sprinted to this little shop in Tunbridge Wells which specifically sold ballet pieces. I had a pink leotard, a matching pink cardigan, pale pink tights and ballet pumps. Obviously, I was cute as fuck.

Our next-door neighbour happened to be the teacher and for a few months, I went to my ballet lessons once a week and low-key thought I was smashing it. Until one day after class, the teacher/next-door neighbour pulled my mum aside and told her that I struggled with the *elegance* that is needed for ballet. She suggested that perhaps ballet wasn't for me. She went on to say that I was a bit heavy footed and that, compared to the other girls, I danced like an "excitable elephant".

My mum was so embarrassed that she never took me back. In fact, it's funny how certain memories stick out in your head because I can vaguely remember my mum answering her: "Ah yeah, fair enough." (Insert eye roll.) "That sounds like our Chloe."

Like cheers Mum.

God bless the nineties. Imagine a teacher saying that to a mum now? She'd be slagged off on Facebook left, right and centre and there'd be a petition to remove her teaching rights for body shaming by the weekend.

To sum up though, I don't feel like "participating" ever did me any favours.

"I'll work on it," I lie.

"You seem to enjoy Art therapy which is great, and I hear from staff members that you're always so polite and you get on well with everyone."

I nod. It's giving out parents' evening vibes now and I can't help but smile. He'll be saying next that I need to stop distracting others.

"How do you feel like you're getting on here?"

Oh god, I hate these questions, I feel like it's a trick.

"I think I'm doing ok. I'm feeling more positive about going to bed and I'm relaxing better in the evenings, but I don't know how my anxiety will cope back in the real world again."

He nods enthusiastically, so I must have said the right thing.

"I think that's a really good observation. It comes to a point here where you need to go back outside so you can progress forward."

Oh shit. I didn't say that did I? Did I suggest I need to be back outside? Because that's not what I meant.

"You won't be able to learn the coping mechanisms for the next stage whilst you are in here, so I think it is really vital that we get you back home as soon as possible. That way, you can start navigating being back out there and learning how to cope with those situations."

What? Is this actually happening?

"How does next weekend sound?"

It's happening.

CHAPTER TWENTY-TWO
IT'S BEEN EMOTIONAL

One girl was discharged before me; she lived in Kent too and it was clear this was good news to her. She didn't look nervous at all, but rather quite eager. I didn't get to know her much, but she was always friendly. She was in for self-harming but in the end, she found a healthier way to cope. She started wearing elastic bands around her wrists and when she felt anxious, she'd ping those instead. Sometimes they'd leave quite a sore-looking raised red bump around her wrist, but I suppose that's still better than actually cutting the skin.

Both Lisa and Katie look gutted when I tell them the news that I'm out of here at the weekend. Of course, they're happy for me but it's like a little dysfunctional family here, you get used to each other and you bond. It's sad when you see someone go, you know you'll miss them.

Apart from Tom of course who just grunts,

"Alright, bye then." When I still have five days to go.

"Wow, Chloe!" Jim beams as he high fives me. "Congratulations. I hope you enjoy the rest of your life."

"No pressure then eh, Jim," I laugh.

"There's no pressure, I already know you're going to do so well. And be successful!" He raises two thumbs up at me with a wide grin.

I try to read how Lisa is feeling but it isn't easy. To be honest, I think for the most part she's fine, I don't think she ever really thought my plan was going to materialise and I'm not sure she even wanted it to. Lisa is very independent, she's had to be. I don't think living under a roof with me and my mum who she barely knows would have been what she wanted at all.

"What are you going to do when you get out, Chlo?" Katie asks. "Are you going to go back to college?"

The thought fills me with dread. I was in college just before I landed here, and I didn't cope well at all. I remember as soon as the classroom door closed in each lesson, I felt a huge amount of dread and anxiety. I felt stuck. I'd count down the minutes until I could leave again. It was a shame because I was studying English Language and Film Studies, and I enjoyed both of those immensely. But my brain and my anxiety couldn't cope with the feeling of being "locked" in a classroom for two hours with twenty other students.

"I don't think so, I'd have to go back in a new term and start all over again. I think I'll do something else for a little while."

My dad agreed that I wouldn't be ready to work for

a while yet but we both know I'll need something else to fill my time otherwise I'll sink again. The overthinking will come back, so will the severe agoraphobia. I'll need a hobby to keep me busy – maybe I'll volunteer at a cat rescue or something.

The rest of my week is fairly uneventful. One evening, we have a very late-night admission, which is something I haven't seen before. It's usually all scheduled when someone new is arriving – I didn't even realise the hospital took emergencies until now. She's a girl of around seventeen who was taken to A&E after apparently threatening to or trying to kill herself. The hospital sent her here to keep her safe temporarily. She's like a bull in a china shop. By one o'clock in the morning, she has everyone out of their bedrooms and skidding down the hallway using their pillowcases. She was the only person I ever met who had as much fun in here as if it was Disney World.

She was gone the next day but still, she briefly livened up the place. Tom was so happy he had a wank. But that doesn't take much.

The next evening, I'm straightening Heather's hair in the communal lounge. She's headed off on a date after work, her first one since her divorce and I'm so happy for her. She watches me work the hair iron through her hair in the mirror and smiles as I do so. It makes me happy that I can help make her feel pretty before the big date. Well, prettier. She's already pretty, and her kind heart makes her beautiful.

"So, Chloe, tell me how you're feeling about going home on Friday?"

"Pretty melancholy if I'm honest." I pronounce the word with too much emphasis on the 'ch' which makes Heather burst out laughing.

"Do you mean melancholy? The H is silent."

For fuck's sake, I've been trying to learn new words instead of always saying *depressed* or *anxious* because I'm so bored with hearing myself say those words over and over again and I thought I'd sound really smart using that word. Never mind.

After Heather giggles and makes a mental note to tell that one in the staffroom later, she gives me a hug and asks me why I'm feeling so *melancholy*.

"I'm scared to try and go back to a normal life. I'm scared that I won't be able to keep up with everyone else, that I'll never be able to hold down a job, so I'll have no money, no prospects. Nothing. I'm scared I'll move back into a house where my dad worries so much that it's stressful for him. *I'm* stressful to be around."

And although I don't say it, I'm scared of seeing the people I used to hang out with. What will all my friends think? I've only been away for four months but in teenage life that can feel like a very long time. What if everyone has moved on without me? Will college boy pester me when I'm out? Will my mum go back to her old ways of 4am phone calls and threats?

It's a lot.

"All of that is normal Chlo…" Heather comforts me, her voice gentle and compassionate. "Just because you're going home on Friday doesn't mean that you're expected to be cured, it's just another step in your journey. And you know you can always come back as an outpatient and spend time with us if you need to."

I'll definitely miss Heather the most, she's been my most comforting person in here and I know throughout life I'll always think about her from time to time. Hoping that she's living the life that she deserves.

This place that I had dreaded has become my home. It hasn't always been plain sailing but for the most part it has given me a great deal of comfort. I have felt so protected from the outside world and now I'm about to rejoin it.

Friday comes around way quicker than I was ready for.

Finally, I get all my belongings back, including my phone, and from this day forward, nobody will need to watch me take a bath.

My dad and stepmum have arrived already and are hovering with the nurses by the staffroom, probably to give me a few minutes to get myself together and say my goodbyes privately.

Tom's first. Well actually, he comes out of his room, rolls his eyes when he realises that I'm still here and then mutters something about goodbyes lasting forever.

Jim comes out, hugging me so tightly that he nearly lifts me off the floor. He is wearing four jumpers today and that's okay; it doesn't mean it's necessarily a bad day, but I know Jim isn't fond of change and me leaving today is definitely a change. "Please be happy Chloe, you deserve to be very, very happy. You are the best lady I have met, and you deserve to be really happy and have only happy things happen to you."

My eyes fill with tears. "Thanks Jim," I manage to say through the lump in my throat. "Don't ever let anyone dull your sparkle."

Which is cheesy but it's true and it's all I can manage to say otherwise I really will start full-on ugly crying. Jim is by far one of life's kindest souls and I hope he is never given a reason to stop seeing the world as beautifully as he does.

Katie is next and I realise now that this is the first day I am seeing her skin back to its normal fair self, no more hints of yellow from that horrific overdose.

"Maybe we can meet up one day, when we are both better?" she whispers into my ear as we hug.

"I'd love that." I smile and take that as hopeful confirmation that Katie has no future plans to overdose again.

Lastly, I turn to give Lisa a hug, but she steps away and sheepishly nods for me to follow her to her room. I look back at my dad who is still in a conversation with the nurses and decide he'll be fine waiting one last minute.

When I get to Lisa's room, she takes out my Lakers jersey from her nightstand and hands it back to me. She asked to borrow it one day; said she loved the NBA and never owned a jersey before. I didn't mind, I literally only bought it because I thought I'd look really gang in it when me and my mates went to Trocadero in London. I can confirm I looked anything other than *gang*.

"Keep it," I say and her face instantly lights up.

"Are you sure?"

"Yep. I look like a twat in it. At least you can actually pull it off."

"Thank you." She throws it behind her on the bed before turning her attention back onto me. "When I get out of here, they'll probably send me back up north to be looked after until they find somewhere more permanent. So, I'm not even sure if I'll see you again, but just in case I don't…"

And then suddenly, Lisa's lips are on mine. She kisses me gently and all I can think is *oh my god*! Did I become Lisa's bitch in here and just not realise? It's giving *Bad Girls* vibes – we're the new Shaz and Denny. What if my dad turns the corner right now? I'd never live it down.

Then she pulls away and I'm just standing there with an expression like Ross in *Friends* when Rachel tells him she's pregnant with their baby.

"I fell for you quite quickly after I met you. So, if you ever find yourself up near where I live, or you know, a lesbian, then you know where I am."

I walk back out of her room and towards my dad feeling like what just happened was SO obvious. Like I was wearing a Rosie O'Donnell t-shirt with Tatu's "All the things she said" playing behind me.

Imagine being mentally ill and still pulling though? Maybe I am a bit gang after all.

CHAPTER TWENTY-THREE
ONE MONTH LATER

"Excuse me?" A petite lady with mousy brown hair stops me on the pavement to my mum's road.

I smile politely although the socially anxious person inside of me is screaming. "Yes?"

"Do you see that house over there?" I follow the lady's pointed finger and see her aiming it in the direction of my mum's house. I'm not too surprised when I see that Mum's house looks a little neglected. The front lawn is so badly overgrown that it's probably four foot high. I haven't been here in a very long time. I came by to see the new house when the incident with Griff wasn't so raw, but I haven't been back since.

"Yeah?" I play dumb. I have no idea what she's about to say but I assume she is going to mention the messy exterior and it'll just be awkward to admit that I know the owner of the house if she's about to go on a rant. Which judging by her frown, she's about to.

"It's disgraceful, isn't it? Our little cul-de-sac was

beautiful before she came along. She has no respect whatsoever for her neighbours and the fact that we try hard to keep our street looking pretty and tidy."

"Hmm-mm."

"We've even offered to cut it for her – my husband went round with his own lawnmower, but she told him to sod off. It's like she enjoys being difficult. At this rate, she'll make our houses drop in value, because who'd want to wake up and look at that eyesore every day?"

I mean, she has a point. Just at that moment, I see my mum glaring through the living room window, watching us. If looks could kill, this woman next to me would be well and truly deceased.

I didn't pay attention at first, but now I notice the woman is holding a clipboard and as I peer over her shoulder, I see the pages are filled with signatures. Oh my god, it's not a… is it?

"So, would you please help us by signing this petition?"

It is! It's a bloody petition that the entire street has been signing just to get my mum to mow her lawn. I find myself biting my bottom lip hard to keep from laughing. This is hilarious. I'm glad to see my mum is just as difficult towards everybody else as she is with her family.

"Sure." I smirk, grabbing the pen and scribbling down my name. I can practically feel my mum's eyes burning into me.

"Thank you, we're really hoping this will be enough to get the council's attention. Perhaps then they can come out and do it and she'll just have to accept it."

"Absolutely. Scruffy cow." I nearly lose it as I say that last part, but I manage to keep my laughter in.

I hand back the clipboard as she smiles and walk quickly past her and straight towards my mum's house. Thankfully the door is unlocked so I just let myself straight in. Just as I close the door behind me, I catch a glimpse of the woman's face, jaw dropped open, looking completely dumbfounded and confused. She certainly didn't expect that.

"Chloe!" My mum appears in the hallway, cigarette in hand. "Did *she* just show you that bloody petition!?"

"Yeah."

"What did you do?"

"Signed it," I say with a little shrug.

"Fuck off! What did you do that for?" she moans before puffing on her cigarette.

"To be fair Mum, it is pretty messy out there. Why haven't you just done it?"

"Can't be bothered. I'm not Charlie Dimmock and it doesn't bother me. So why should I break my back out there for hours?"

"Well, they're your neighbours?"

"And? This is how it starts Chloe, first they ask you to trim your garden and before you know it, they're asking you to chip in for the whip round for number 10's new hip. I'm absolutely not doing it."

I spend the next hour listening to Mum basically telling me that all her neighbours are plotting to take her down and that she hates them. This is the first time I've seen her since I left the hospital. I thought it was best to drop in because sadly a close friend to Mum passed away and I was worried she'd be really struggling.

But she pretty much seems herself.

Last time my mum went to a funeral, she picked out a huge black 'statement' hat for the actual ceremony which was basically a black sombrero and got so drunk at the pub that she passed out in the car park in a puddle of her own vomit.

"Did you hear I'm not allowed to go to the funeral?"

"I hadn't heard Mum, no, but it's not really a surprise is it?"

"What do you mean? Because I think it's a bloody liberty!"

"It is, I understand that, but over the last few years you've sent funeral brochures to everyone you don't like, you tried hiring somebody to hurt Dad, you abandoned the family cat, you got me arrested, oh and the last funeral you went to? You played The Monkees' "I'm a believer" like five times on the jukebox."

"It wasn't *five*! And anyway, I was trying to get everybody up and dancing because they were all so bloody miserable." She stares at me blankly, not looking the least bit affected by any of her other behaviour that I've listed off. "And anyway, Griff was free to roam in a five-bedroom detached house Chloe, I'd say he was a pretty lucky cat…"

"Not without food he wasn't."

"Oh god, cats are hunters Chlo, that's what they do, they go and get their own food."

"Yeah, not when they're fucking locked in though Mum."

She rolls her eyes at me as if I'm the one being dramatic.

"Anyway…" she changes the subject. "How's that girl? Lisa? The one you wanted me to move in here." She says Lisa's name just like she says my dad's – like it leaves a sour taste in her mouth, and I don't appreciate it.

"I don't know."

"What do you mean you *don't* know?"

"I haven't been back to the hospital since I came home."

"Why not? I thought they said you could be an outpatient."

"Yes, but I didn't want to. Once I was home again, properly, it just felt like it would be too weird to keep going back."

"Oh right, so you don't know whether her own mother sorted her out with a home or not?"

"No, I'm trying to concentrate on myself. That's what my therapist said I needed to do."

"Just a bit weird that you wanted me to save the day so bad, making out she was your best ever friend and now you don't even know what she's up to."

I can feel the tone in her voice changing which causes my defences to quickly go back up.

"Just leave it, Mum."

"What did your *father* have to say about it all anyway?" Again, the word 'father' comes out like it's a disgusting word.

"Nothing, really. Just forget about it."

She gives me a fully judgemental look that makes me feel stupid all over again like I did at the time. Which frustrates the hell out of me because I chose to put it all behind me. Once I realised Lisa had feelings for me on top of everything else, it just seemed even clearer that I needed to pull away. Dr Pope said that I needed to be as stress free as possible, particularly when I first got home. He said it would be a difficult transition, and I needed to keep my mind clear from anything unhelpful.

And I fully intend doing just that. I'm tired of feeling like the oldest seventeen-year-old in the world because I don't go out and I avoid experiencing anything new. I have to put myself first.

"Instead, why don't you catch me up on things that have been happening here?"

"Oh god, Chloe, where do I start?" she says, lighting another cigarette.

I flop down on the sofa next to her, fighting the second-hand smoke.

"Your sister is a single mum now."

"What!? What happened?"

"He left her didn't he? On his mate's stag weekend in Zante, ended up getting it on with the holiday rep and now he's moved in with her."

Holiday rep? How cliché.

"That's awful though Mum. Is she ok?"

"Who?"

"My sister?"

"Oh right, yeah! I guess so, I think she had a few

breakdowns and got a bit upset. She said he was the scum of the earth. I thought *that's* a bit far. He's not that bad, I always liked him. Thought he was a right laugh."

"Well, I guess when he cheated and left her with a baby, she didn't find him that funny anymore."

"Yeah, shame."

Unfortunately, we didn't seem to have a whole lot to talk about after that. I thought she might ask if I wanted to stay for dinner, maybe even offer to get a takeaway, anything really that could be a positive step forward for the both of us, but she did no such thing. I texted Dad not long after and asked him to pick me up.

Looking back, I think Mum was still grieving for her marriage, which made her self-centred and appear really unloving. I don't think she thought to ask me about my life because in her mind, nobody else's troubles could even compare to what she'd been through the last few years. Some women just don't *get over* relationships well, I learned.

CHAPTER TWENTY-FOUR
IT'S LIKE I NEVER LEFT.

I haven't really had the opportunity to meet face-to-face with many friends yet. I've spoken to a couple of my closest friends on the phone but nothing else.

"You should come to Melissa's house party!" Kiki says for at least the fifth time.

"I don't know. Do you think so? I feel like I'll be really boring – I won't drink much, and I'll probably go to bed by like midnight."

We've been on the phone together now for over an hour which is pretty normal for us. Kiki knows I want to stay in a healthy sleep routine and the idea of going out to house parties or sleepovers is making me a bit worried.

"That's fine. If you go to bed, then I'll come with you. It's not like anyone will have a problem with it, they understand that you're doing what you need to."

I hesitate. I want to say yes because I'd love to be that seventeen-year-old girl. The one who can go hang out at parties and be a bit more carefree. But I also know that only a couple of months ago I was very unwell, and I don't ever want to be back there again.

"How about this, if you feel like it's too much at any time, I'll get my mum to pick us up and we'll just crash at my place? You know she's always happy to come get us whenever."

Kiki's mum is young, easy-going and funny. We all love her – it's almost as though she's one of us. Just a bit older. She's a good mum but since she was so young when she had Kiki, they seem more like friends, and I was always a little jealous of that. Whenever I'd go to Kiki's house for a sleepover, Kiki and her mum would always be in the back garden sitting in these little deckchairs smoking cigarettes and drinking cups of coffee, discussing this, that and everything in between. She was one of the cool mums who didn't seem to mind her daughter smoking or even drinking alcohol within reason even though we weren't quite eighteen. She was fun and easy to talk to. But she also worked hard – she was a single mum to Kiki and her little brother, working full time and also training to be a nurse. She was a superwoman.

"Ok, alright then," I eventually agree.

"Yes! I'm so excited to finally PARTAY with my best friend! It's been forever."

***

Akon blares in the background, our glasses are filled with either blue WKD or cheap Lambrini and the vibes are good. There are just five of us girls; we've been friends since year seven at school and they are all so happy to see me. Nobody has really asked any questions either. Only if I'm feeling better. Which I am. I mean, I'm out, at a house party, something which is feeling huge but also easy at the same time. I feel like a typical seventeen-year-old.

We sing along to songs, dance, update our Bebo, Myspace and Facebook profiles. We take a hundred photos on Melissa's pink Canon camera. It is shaping up to be a really fun night.

"Ah, the boys will be here soon," Melissa announces, staring down at the screen on her phone.

"Boys?"

"Yeah, your besties!" she says with a huge grin.

I haven't seen my two friends from college since they came to visit me at the hospital and were scared off by Tom and his wank-a-thon in my bedroom. I didn't judge them at all for not coming back – it wasn't exactly the easiest environment to be in if you weren't used to it.

Around five minutes later, I hear a quiet knock on the front door. It seems like nobody else has heard it and since I already know it's the boys, I go to let them in.

Adam gives me the brightest smile as soon as I open the door. It's like he is so proud and relieved to see me standing in front of him, back in the outside world and not in the unit. He pulls me in for the tightest hug. "It's so good to see you back where you belong, Chlo."

Behind him is Matty who gives me a wink and a smile. A little gesture but I know he is letting me know he is also proud of me for getting well enough to come back home.

But then, lurking behind Matty, with a hood up and a cigarette hanging out of his mouth, I see college boy. My stomach drops into my arse. Literally.

What is *he* doing here? I almost want to cry and demand answers but then I remember that I didn't tell anyone about him. The only person in this house who has any idea is Kiki. And even she doesn't know the full extent. We've chatted on the phone a lot since I've been home and I told her that I broke up with him, that I'd had time to reflect and realise that he wasn't good for me. She agreed. She said she picked up on some red flags and thought he was a bit controlling, but she has *no idea* about the video, the threats, the manipulation. None of it.

When his eyes meet mine, they're dark and cold. His mouth moves into a disgusted smirk and then he lets out a quiet humph beneath his breath but loud enough for me to hear. He's trying to intimidate me – the way he is standing, the hood up, the glare, the rolling of the cigarette between his fingertips like a fucking Kray twin. Everything he is subtly doing right now is for my benefit.

I turn quickly on my heel and go to find Kiki whilst the boys greet Melissa and hand her another bottle of WKD that they probably got at the shop along the way.

"He's here!" I whisper when I find Kiki outside smoking with Jess and Megan.

She knows who I mean straight away and her eyes

widen. She flicks her cig over the fence and charges into the house.

Oh no, she's going to kick off. I'm hot on her tail but she's too quick. She bursts into the kitchen where Melissa is making all three lads a drink.

"You can stay away from Chloe, you freak! Just because you're in the same house as her, don't think for a single second I'm going to let you upset her!"

Everyone looks a bit taken aback, except for college boy who looks like he was expecting this.

His eyes look me and Kiki up and down and he lets out a very unkind snigger.

"I don't know what you're talking about Kiki. I don't associate with people who've been in the nuthouse, so I planned to stay well away from that anyway."

"Hey!" Adam intervenes. "Come on man, there's no need for that."

He smirks and shrugs, like he's said absolutely nothing untoward. "Oh, come on, you're all thinking it! That's why you and Matty didn't go back to visit – you were embarrassed! You told me."

Adam and Matty instantly protest. "No, we didn't quite say that. We said it was awkward, yeah, especially after that day with that Tom guy, but we didn't say Chloe was embarrassing…"

"Yeah, yeah."

"It's true. Don't be a dick, man…"

He just nods as if they're talking shit to cover their tracks. He's so clever at making me doubt stuff like that. Doubt whether people are telling the truth, whether people really like me or not. It's a horrible feeling that brings back all the uncertainty and knocks my confidence.

With that realisation, I know it's time to call it a night. There is no way I'll waste any more time with him and give him any more opportunities to get inside my head.

CHAPTER TWENTY-FIVE
IT'S GIVING SLEEP PARALYSIS DEMON

Kiki follows me up to bed quite soon after. She sits and reassures me that nobody is embarrassed of me. And then eventually, after chatting about lighter topics, we fall asleep.

It's about two o'clock in the morning when I stir and notice quickly that Kiki is no longer lying in the bed next to me. I sit up and peer out of the window, seeing that Kiki is now outside with Jess having a cigarette. Maybe she woke up because of all the noise downstairs – the music had been loud and she must have decided to join them for a bit. I decide to just turn back over and get comfy, she'll come back up when she's ready. And then, as soon as it's morning, I'll be texting my dad to come and pick me up and getting the hell out of here.

But that's when I hear *him* clear his throat from across the room. I lean up on my elbow and peer over the duvet. I see college boy sitting on the floor by the door, arms propped up on his knees, staring at me in the dark.

"What are you doing in here!?"

"Er, you're not the only one who needs peace and quiet princess. I have a headache, came up to chill."

"Can't you chill in another room!?"

"Not really. They're all being used. Relax, it's not like we've not spent plenty of nights together before."

I feel sick at the memory.

I lie frozen in the bed. I don't know whether to bang on the window for Kiki to come back up, storm out of the house and attempt to walk home, which will probably take me like six hours, or just ignore him, pretend I don't care and force myself back to sleep.

"Scooch over and we'll have a cuddle." His voice breaks the silence once more.

"No thanks."

After a very brief pause, he laughs again, but in that unkind way that makes me nervous.

"I really pity you, do you know that?"

I don't answer.

"I had to beg Melissa to let you come to this party."

I don't answer. I've known Melissa for six years. He only met her through me. Melissa is *my* friend.

"And for what it's worth, Adam and Matty *were* really embarrassed and ashamed to be your friend after that incident at the hospital. They came home and told me all about it. We all laughed. They just won't admit it because they're worried that you'll freak out on them."

I don't answer. Adam is one of my favourite people.

I knew him before I knew college boy. He's a good guy. He's been a good friend.

"As for your dad, I really did hear him say those things about you. That you're a burden."

I don't answer.

"And a strain on the family as well as putting a scary amount of stress on his heart. And that's not good for someone who had a heart attack is it? Was it one heart attack? Or two?"

I still don't answer. I don't give him the satisfaction of getting a reaction. I am stronger than this now. If I can battle a mental illness every day, then I can deal with him.

And I do.

CHAPTER TWENTY-SIX

I'm telling my mum on you.

Ok, so I may have given myself a little too much credit there, because *I* didn't do anything. I left the room and found Kiki and together we managed to sleep on the sofa for an hour or two. We also left before everybody else woke up. Including college boy.

But I was so proud. I didn't rise to the bait. I didn't lose my head, I didn't let him get to me and best of all, I didn't let him make me cry again.

But I was done with keeping everything bottled up. I phoned my mum and told her everything. Well, *almost* everything. I still couldn't bring myself to talk about the video, but I did tell her about the threats, about the messages he'd send at two or three in the morning, the things he'd tell me about how I was a burden, all of it.

"Him?" Mum said down the phone. "But he looks like fucking Harry Potter."

He did look like Harry Potter to be fair. But just

because he looks like a fictional boy wizard doesn't mean he isn't actually a sociopath.

"Right, well I'll handle this one, Chloe, leave it with me."

Now, in hindsight, this maybe wasn't my best idea. I'd kind of hoped Mum would just get drunk one evening and start ringing *him*, singing her best ABBA renditions down the phone, because I know only too well how fast that gets tiresome. However, it's Carol. She doesn't do things by halves.

She did something much worse.

Now, obviously, I think I should make it clear that I am a totally innocent and upstanding member of society. Clearly. Mum, however…

It had been three weeks and to be honest I had forgotten all about the fact I'd told Mum. She hadn't said whether she phoned him or did anything, so I assumed she forgot. One evening I was having dinner at my sister's house when Mum turned up. She was in quite a good mood and offered to take us to ASDA to get some snacks and drinks for a movie night. It was the first time in years I had heard Mum offer to do something so genuine and kind. There were no ulterior motives here. Nothing to do with Dad. Just an offer to spend time with her daughters. We both jumped at the offer.

But on the drive back from ASDA, we seemed to be doing a detour. Mum was driving straight to college boy's house.

That's when I noticed the bag of flour on my sister's

lap in the front seat. Flour isn't exactly a typical movie snack.

"Mum?" I asked suspiciously from the backseat.

"Don't worry, they'll never know it's you."

Firstly, thank the Lord this happened before every Tom, Dick and Sally had a Ring doorbell. Secondly, my mum has just parked us up right outside his fucking house. Not exactly inconspicuous.

I'm sitting in the backseat like a rabbit caught in the headlights. I have no idea what's going to happen.

She grabs the bag of flour and heads straight to their driveway. It's dark so I can't see exactly what she's doing but she appears to be carefully orchestrating the flour. So maybe it's a picture or a word.

I'm panicking big time. I'm not cut out for this. My mum of course used to come to my dad's house regularly to slash his tyres and smash windows with plant pots, so she does this like it's second nature. Not an ounce of fear in her. So much so that she is really taking her time, not at all concerned as to whether anyone is home or if anyone is about to catch her. She looks down at the ground, her brows bunched together. I can see her sounding out a word to herself. I wonder what word she's been writing.

"Hey! she calls back to the car in a whisper-shout. "Is there an E in cunt?"

"No!" my sister answers for me. "It's just C-U-N-T."

Mum looks satisfied and carries on with the final letter.

Great, she's writing 'cunt' on my ex-boyfriend's driveway.

My sister giggles. My heart beats so loud I can hear it in my ears.

I expect Mum to come walking back to the car after she finishes the T, but she doesn't. She proudly inspects her handiwork and then heads straight to the front door of their house, opens up the flap to their letterbox and yells: "Tell your weird son that if he harasses my daughter again, the next time I'll be tattooing it on his fucking forehead."

Then, without a single care in the world, she takes a leisurely stroll back to the car and we drive off.

"The good thing about flour Chlo is that it's fairly easy to wash away, so it doesn't class as criminal damage. I learned that when I met this woman outside the police station when your dad had me arrested. Helpful tip. You're welcome."

I'm not condoning what my mum did. She has always been fiery, a lot like my nan apparently, although she died when I was just two years old, so I had never met her. But my mum used to say that although she was hilarious, she was a hot head and would do pretty drastic things when she lost her temper. So, I guess in this scenario, the apple really doesn't fall far from the tree.

But, in a strange way, this made me feel closer to my mum. I felt like this was her way of saying *I love you* and *I'm not perfect, but I'll always have your back*. Although the act of what she did may not be something I'd recommend, the sentiment behind it meant something.

And because of that, as we drove home, I felt this little glimmer of hope that me and Mum may well be turning a corner, finally.

CHAPTER TWENTY-SEVEN
VIVA ESPANA

I needed a change. I needed adventure. But mostly, I needed to *live*.

I had been spending most nights at Kiki's house, well, I'd practically moved in. Another friend from school who has been in our friendship circle since forever had also moved in. So, under one roof were Kiki's mum and little brother, then Kiki, me and our other best friend Bow.

Both the girls worked around thirty hours a week, Kiki at Sports Direct and Bow at Waitrose. I still didn't have a job. Even the thought made me panic to the point I thought I might hyperventilate. It's hard to really describe why it seemed so scary to me, because I'm not a lazy person. In fact, I do better in a routine and being out of the house, I think it helps my mental health and stops me from developing agoraphobia again. However, there's this feeling of being *trapped* that makes me panic most.

Jobs inside shopping centres are a real no-go because then I'm in a building that's *in* a building, which means my exit is even further away. I also struggle with committing myself to being in one place for four to nine hours a day, because what if I have a panic attack after one hour? Then what? What if I have to run out of the shop or office in front of everybody? It's not just the fear of embarrassment that gives me anxiety, but also the feeling of letting other staff down because I'm a flight risk.

To sum up, my brain wasn't ready for that quite yet. So my dad was paying my keep towards my stay at Kiki's as well as pinging me over money here and there when I needed it. I also sold my little Ford Fiesta that Dad had got me before I got unwell. Obviously, I wasn't ready to drive either, so I let that go and put the seven hundred pounds I made from it in a little savings pot.

The girls and I were bored but mostly really uninspired. We just didn't know what to do anymore. A lot of our friends had gone to university and were continuing to strive towards a career. But Kiki, Bow and I had no idea what career we wanted. Does anyone at that age?

So, after a night of debating and sharing ideas, we ended up with the absolutely foolproof plan of moving to Spain. Bow's dad lived in Valencia so if we got really stuck, he could help us.

But we wouldn't need help because, as I said, it was foolproof. I'd take my savings; the girls would take their last pay-check and together we'd go out and find bar work. Bow and Kiki were already eighteen and I would be eighteen next month. So that wouldn't be too much of a problem. We'd quickly find a villa, one with a private pool. It'd be modern and gorgeous, and everyone would want to come and visit us to see how well we were all doing. We'd be working at night and sunbathing during the day. The sun would give us that golden glow and a tonne of vitamin D – we'd literally be the epitome of good health and happiness. Our lives would officially change for the better. Oh yes, Spain was the answer to all our problems.

It's important to note that on our first night in Benidorm, we saw an old man with his pants down, having a wank outside a KFC. Definitely not quite the glamorous Spain we envisioned. But we'll get to that later.

I was on Facebook one night, sitting with the girls, planning life in Spain when I was "poked" by a man I recognised but hadn't seen in a long time.

Now poking on Facebook to get somebody's attention probably started out completely innocently, but circa 2008, it definitely meant *hello, I fancy you, I'd quite like to bang you please.* The guy in question was somebody I'd met in a pub a year ago. He was only a couple of years older than me and I'd always got the impression he fancied me a bit, but I had a boyfriend at the time. We'll call this guy Jay and it's important to note that Jay ended up becoming the biological father to my first born. But that's years away yet, so we won't get into that too much now.

Anyway, I knew that Jay had moved away but it was only now, after his *poking,* that I learned that he had moved to Murcia, Spain, with his parents. We sent messages back and forth and eventually, he and his mum invited us to stay in their villa for a little while. They had three spare bedrooms and although they said they lived somewhere quite rural, the girls and I thought it could be a really good stopgap while we found some work and saved more money before heading into Benidorm. We seized the opportunity and booked our EasyJet flights. In a few days' time, we'd be touching down in Alicante!

Now my dad obviously had a lot of concerns over this idea – it was only a little while ago I was in a hospital. It's crazy when I actually think back to how scary this must have been for him. I'd gone from one extreme to the next – from being in a secure unit, watched twenty-four-seven, to suddenly flying off to another country where my only supervision would be by two eighteen-year-old girls.

I went for a lunch with my dad the day before we flew to Spain and had a very emotional heart-to-heart. He just wanted me to be happy, but he was worried for me, and if I was being honest, I was worried for myself. But I felt like I needed to do something wild, to prove to myself that I could. More than anything, I wanted to make up for lost time. I'd had years of life being such a struggle, always cancelling things, coming home early or not going at all. I was finally now in a decent headspace where I felt like I could *do* things, and I could *go* places. I was excited to go for it.

Isn't it funny how some memories just stick with

you as clear as day? I remember everything about that day at Gatwick as we waited to board our plane, even what I was wearing: a cute yellow halter-neck top and blue denim shorts. I went to WH Smith and got a bottle of water and a magazine. Everything was smooth sailing. Well, almost everything – my suitcase had broken the night before and Kiki's mum had to dig out a replacement from the loft. It wasn't a drag along suitcase with wheels. It was closer to a briefcase. It was large and boxy with just one handle to carry it. It looked like something a child would carry when fleeing London in World War Two. Of course, the girls ripped the piss.

Where'd you get your bag, Heartbeat? (Which was a TV show that was set in the early 60s in case you didn't know.)

Did you steal that bag from the set of Goodnight Mr Tom?

What stinks of mothballs and repels men? Chloe's bag.

So yeah, you get the idea.

But before we knew it, we three girls had touched down in Alicante in the scorching humid heat of late July. And it was glorious. This was the Spanish sun we'd been dreaming about.

Jay and his mum came to meet us from the airport, which I remember at the time was pretty nerve-wrecking.

"If you're wondering why we're late, we had to wait for Chloe's bag to arrive from 1942," Kiki joked, immediately breaking the ice although making me totally red in the face in front of Jay.

Both Jay and his mum were pleasant and welcoming, and we were really grateful to have somebody waiting for us at the other end. It felt a little less daunting knowing this.

The villa was truly beautiful, as was the area, but they weren't kidding when they said it was rural. There was one little bar a ten-minute walk away and that was it. Everything else, shops, restaurants, supermarkets, was a half-hour drive away. Which meant that any hopes of part-time work were gone – we didn't have a car, buses didn't come this way and a taxi would have been very expensive. And obviously, this tiny local bar didn't need three bar girls, especially when its clientele consisted of about seven people.

We tried to be patient and see if we could make it work because the place really was truly stunning. The villa overlooked a vineyard, the skies were blue every day, the sun was hot and the small number of locals were friendly enough. We were grateful to be here, but we couldn't ignore the fact that we were slowly getting cabin fever. We'd been doing the same thing now for three weeks. It had become *Groundhog Day*: get up, swim, sunbathe, look for jobs with no luck and repeat.

Instead of making money, we were slowly eating into our savings with nothing to show.

We knew we had to go somewhere with more options. That place was Benidorm.

CHAPTER TWENTY-EIGHT
BENIDORM 2008 BABY!

Without any plans or arrangements for the other side, the girls and I leave Murcia on a coach late one night. We have to wait a few hours for our second coach from Alicante to Benidorm, which means by the time we make it to Benidorm it is close to four o'clock in the morning.

Stag and hen parties are rife. We don't really have a clue what to do or where to go so we just sit with our luggage by the beach, waiting for sunrise. After some time, we start attracting a fair amount of unwanted attention from drunk lads – I guess three girls sitting with suitcases stick out like a sore thumb. Bow suggests we go and sit in a McDonald's or KFC since they're twenty-four hours.

That's when we find the old man sitting outside on the bench having a vigorous wank. I wonder if he knew Tom.

Our first impression of Benidorm is definitely an interesting one! It's certainly a far cry from Murcia.

As the sun slowly comes up, we go from hotel to hotel trying to find one with a room. Benidorm gets very hot very quickly and after a sleepless night on coaches, we are beyond shattered. After a couple of hours walking around, pulling suitcases, we eventually find a little three-star hotel opposite the Red Lion pub. Perfect. We make a plan to sleep and then head over the road for a full English breakfast. Once we are refreshed and energised, we can get job-hunting.

I remember trying to fall asleep in the hotel but finding that the excitement and nervousness were making it difficult. Plus, I could hear people from the window down by the pool, laughing and playing, enjoying their holiday and it made me all the more pumped to get going.

Eventually, I drift off and wake a few hours later with Bow and Kiki. All of us are feeling a little more alive and raring to go.

Benidorm looks much better during the day. Once the stags and hens are off the street and presumably in bed sleeping off their hangovers, the town becomes mostly families. Lots of parents with small children are heading down to the beach, carrying towels and inflatables on their shoulders. A fair few couples who look to be newly retired are sitting outside pubs enjoying a drink and a cigarette under the sunshine. Yeah, it's definitely a lot less intimidating now than it had been several hours ago.

We make it to an estate agents and find a possible flat. We explain that we don't have jobs yet but we do have savings; she says the landlord will probably be ok with that and we should go meet and talk with him.

It takes us three hours to find this place – we walk and walk and walk some more. In the end, I feel like we've gone so far, I'm not sure I'll be able to find my way back to the main town.

We eventually come to a high-rise block of flats that look, well, grubby to say the least. Our potential flat is on the seventh floor and there's no lift. The flat itself is a tiny two-bedroom unit with not many windows and very little natural light, a very compact kitchen/living room and no air conditioning. It's dark AF.

The landlord wants us to sign a contract to commit to this place for a whole year – and the cost is one thousand euros a month, bills not included. For 2008, this is very expensive. I look back now and wonder if that was the real price or whether he just saw three young and naïve girls and thought he could get more money out of us.

The three of us stand there in this tiny stuffy living room trying to work out the maths in our heads. The minimum wage around this time in Spain is £5.70 an hour. There is no way we can afford this, with bills and food on top.

I am way too scared to admit this though, and Bow and Kiki certainly don't want to tell the pushy landlord that it is too expensive for us, so we pretend to love it and tell him we need to go to the ATM for the deposit. Then we do a runner.

We walk back to the hotel in defeat, checking our bank balances at the ATM on the way back. None of us has much left. Feeding ourselves each day, plus coaches and other essentials for the last few weeks in Murcia mean that we'll be lucky to afford a shed at this rate. I don't want to give up though – this could all turn around, we just need jobs and I'm sure we can find something cheaper. Before we flew out, my dad had found a small villa near Benidorm's old town for 450 euros. That would be way more affordable. We just need to find those.

But the girls aren't as enthusiastic as I am. We start bickering more as the stress of trying to make our dreams a reality overwhelms us. I feel like I have to keep persuading them that this is still a good idea, but I think they lost their spark for the idea a while ago. By the time we get back to the hotel, Kiki and Bow are really quiet. We sit on our beds, on our phones, ignoring each other for a good hour.

"Ok, I propose an idea," Bow eventually sits up and says, breaking the silence. "I think we should treat the next few days as a holiday, go out, have fun, blow what little money we have left and then we'll go to my dad's in Valencia for a bit and sort out our flights home."

Kiki practically jumps off the bed. "Yes! I am so up for that!"

Now in hindsight, I probably should have just said yes. I could have really let my hair down, made memories and had an awesome time. There is no shame in it when things don't quite go to plan. I could have gone back home, saved up again and tried at another time but with much better preparation.

However, that isn't who I am. I am somebody who can't give up. Realistically, I don't think I'll ever get the chance to save money again – I am terrified of getting a job in England. But in Spain, doing casual bar work with my two friends, that feels a whole lot easier. That's what I want and what I feel like I can achieve.

I need this and I don't want to lose the girls. It is gutting to learn we aren't all on the same page anymore.

"Why don't we save our money for just one more day and see if we can get jobs tonight?"

They look at each other without saying a word but it's obvious they aren't interested anymore.

"I just don't think it's worth it." Kiki speaks first. "I just want to have fun."

Bow nods in agreement. "Yeah, and there's no way I'm going to skint myself to live in a flat like the one we saw today."

"No, no, that guy was trying to rip us off. There is so much better out there! We just need to look."

"Nah, I think I just want to have fun now. We've had no luck since we got to Spain. The way I see it, we can keep trying, run out of money and go home anyway or we can at least have some fun and then go home."

I want to cry and protest but I can see they've made up their minds. This plan was never going to be easy, but I am so gutted it has seemingly come to an end.

"Ok…" I say, but not really knowing if I mean it. I've been on a high for weeks since we came out here, I've been so ready to make amazing things happen and now I feel so low.

"The only problem is, when I spoke to my dad, he said he only has room for two of us… And since he knows Kiki already, he'd prefer if I chose her to stay."

Wait, what? I don't know if I buy it. Surely a grown adult man who is a father couldn't be so mean that he'd happily leave one teenage girl to fend for herself in Benidorm. Unless… Unless this is her decision. Maybe she's had enough of me? Maybe I've been pushing this so much that I've become annoying. But surely a real friend wouldn't leave me behind.

"Then what do I do?"

Bow shrugs. "I don't know. Go back to Jay's? He's your *boyfriend* isn't he? He has a big enough villa. Go make your dream happen down there."

I hate that she suggests that, knowing how hard it was to do anything in very rural Murcia. She knows it just as well as I do.

I'll have to get two coaches back down there by myself. My dad would be having kittens if he knew. He told us girls to stick together at all times. So did Kiki's mum. And now we're discussing splitting up, just like that.

"If I do that, I'll need to keep what money I have left. So, if you guys are definitely going to Valencia in a couple of days then I should probably leave now? And go back to Jay's. I can't afford to go partying."

"Well, we are definitely going to Valencia in a couple of days."

"And I definitely can't come? I'll sleep on the sofa? I don't mind?"

"Sorry." Bow shrugs again. "He said no."

Before I know it, I've phoned Jay, crying. I feel like I've lost my friends and I'm not even sure how it happened. I guess we wanted different things in the end, but I never imagined we'd be parting like this.

Whilst the girls get ready for a night out in Benidorm, I am at the coach station alone with a one-way ticket to Murcia via Alicante. I should arrive there by midnight-ish, depending on how long the wait is again at Alicante.

The girls and I have agreed to meet back at Alicante Airport in four or five days and fly home together. Bow wants to spend time with her dad, so she has told me she will let me know when she is ready and which flight to book.

Only the next time I hear from either Bow or Kiki, they're both back in England – without me.

CHAPTER TWENTY-NINE
UN-PANIC ATTACK, POR FAVOR

The journey back to Murcia is eventful. Of course it is. I am by myself now, it just had to happen that way. I bump into a rowdy bunch of football fans who ask me who my favourite football team is out of Barcelona or Madrid. But their tone sounds a little more threatening than I am comfortable with. I know I have to guess the right team otherwise they'll be jeering and giving me grief for the rest of this coach journey no doubt.

It was quite scary looking back. I was sitting at the back of the coach when they got on. They immediately came towards me, kneeling up on their seats, right in my face, shouting something in Spanish. Followed by a middle finger. I soon realised one of them was shouting *Pepe*, but angrily. I couldn't for the life of me remember who Pepe fucking played for so that wasn't much help. And these men, whether they meant to be or not, were quite intimidating. Where's Angela when you need her?

I mean honestly, you couldn't write it. After a shitty day, I've ended up travelling alone on a coach through the night with a huge football rivalry kicking off.

"Madrid o Barcelona, Madrid o Barcelona?!" the man keeps loudly repeating in my face, pushing for an answer. Now if only I had paid attention in Geography, I might have been able to remember which city is closest to us and take an educated guess from that. Fuck it.

"Barcelona!" I say, with chest. Because, why not?

He studies me for a second before a huge smile spreads across his face as he seemingly beams with pride that somebody else appreciates his team. "Si, Si! Barcelona!" For the rest of the journey, I get to listen to Spanish football chants. I can't remember any of them, but I do know they hated Pepe. So yeah, fuck you Pepe.

When I arrive back at the villa, Jay seems really happy to see me, but I feel so down. I cry when I tell him all about how hard it was and how the girls lost interest and how I don't know what to do anymore. This whole idea had given me the most excitement in years and now I don't know what to do with myself. Obviously, he doesn't have all the answers, but he listens all the same. He tells me that his mum has gone back to England to visit family for a week, so the villa is extra quiet at the moment. Apart from crickets, you don't hear a single noise out here.

The next couple of days, I try to distract myself with happier things. I explore more of the local towns, check out the flea markets and beaches, but no matter what I do, I'm still hoping deep down that after having some space and time at Bow's dad's house, the girls might change their minds. Maybe they'll come back here to the villa and we can think of a plan B.

When I wake up on my third day back from Benidorm, I feel a little out of sorts. Jay says it is likely that I'm acclimatising to the heat – apparently, he went through similar after living here for a month and it made him feel a bit headachy and like he was coming down with something. It could be that, but it could also be the stress. I try not to let my health anxiety run away with me though. After all, tomorrow is my birthday – I will finally be turning eighteen.

Texts are starting to come through from my family already.

Hey baby!

Just checking in, are you still having a nice time? Any luck on the job front yet?

The big eighteen tomorrow. I'll send you some cash in the morning. Treat yourself.

Love, Dad x

18 in the morning, sis!
I'll call you tomorrow x

26djnx x pjusa h9o
(From Mum, who later called because she still can't work out how to text.)

That evening, I sit at the computer with a glass of non-alcoholic sangria and upload some pictures to Facebook of the sights I've seen. A few are of me and the girls when we first arrived in Benidorm but mostly, they are of the views I've seen in Murcia, like the vineyard and mountains. That's when I get a phone call from Melissa. I assume she is about to wish me a happy birthday for tomorrow.

"Hey!" I answer the phone quite cheerfully; it is nice to hear from another friend.

"Hey! Where are you?" I can hear lots of noise in the background – music, whispering, giggling.

"I'm in Murcia still, why? What you up to?"

"Nothing, just got some friends over."

I think I hear a familiar voice. "Who?" I ask, but I'm worried I already know.

"Oh, just the usual…" her tone is different too. It's unkind, it's bitchy, it's not at all what I was expecting. "Jess, Megan, Ali… oh and Bow and Kiki." And then there's an eruption of laughter.

"I don't understand? They flew home?"

"YES!" I hear one of them shout in the background. "*We* came back to England. Do I need to spell it out for you?"

I feel like I've been kicked in the stomach and desperately try to hold back the tears as it dawns on me that they just *left me*. How could they? Why would they? I'd never do that to anyone.

"But, why?" I ask, although I don't think anyone really hears me over the giggling.

"Have fun in shitty Murcia!" someone shouts before the phone goes dead.

To this day, I still don't know what went wrong and

why they left me. I know that they found Murcia to be a dead-end and maybe our planning was awful considering that by the time we made it to Benidorm our money was so low. Maybe they were frustrated. Maybe they blamed me for that. Maybe they were mad that I didn't want to stay and party with them. But I couldn't because where else would I go after? I couldn't go to Valencia with them.

So many thoughts race through my mind. I'm not a confident flyer, which they know, and now I'll have to somehow fly home alone. The thought gives me anxiety. It all does. The plans, the girls, being separated – it is all too much and before I know it, I am feeling ten times worse than earlier.

I lay on the sofa, trying to calm myself down. I feel boiling hot, my hands are clammy and my vision is blurry. I feel like my breath isn't going all the way back into my lungs properly. I start getting really light-headed and although logically it should make sense that this is a panic attack, my brain is telling me that something really bad is happening. I am feeling 'out of it' which I will later learn is something called dissociation but at the time I thought I was dying. I feel like my body is giving up on me.

Fortunately, Jay finds me and calls an ambulance which, given how rural we are, takes a good half an hour to get to us. I still felt horrendous when it arrives.

One old man jumps out of the ambulance and comes into the house to see me.

Ah Juan, just the Juan I wanted to see. – A Del-boy Trotter reference bounces into my brain.

He doesn't speak English and my Spanish is abysmal so we really can't communicate well so he just ushers me into the back of the ambulance.

"How come there's only one man?" I ask Jay.

"In the rural areas, they only have one. He drives and then if the patient deteriorates, he pulls over to help them and then carries on driving when he can."

What the hell? Imagine the person is dying – how the hell do you help and drive at the same time? I don't know why but the thought makes me giggle – maybe it's my nerves, but the whole thing sounds like some spoof comedy skit.

I am also being hilariously thrown around in the back of this ambulance like you wouldn't believe. That's another thing about the Spanish that I've learned – they're not too concerned with speed limits. I'll be lucky if I don't turn up at the hospital with an added concussion and a fractured elbow.

We thankfully arrive safely at a very clean, modern-looking hospital. I am feeling a little calmer – or I was until a huge bug crawled along the floor in the waiting room and a nurse came by and squashed it under her trainer, shooting green and yellow guts everywhere. At which point, I nearly fucking pass out. No clue what type of bug produces that by the way, but it was huge.

I don't have to wait too long at all before I am seen by a doctor who speaks great English. He does a couple of observations, like taking my blood pressure and listening to my heart. Then he says the words I knew he was likely to say. "Do you suffer with anxiety?"

Oh god, let's not pull at that thread. We'll be here all night.

But I nod and tell him I do.

"Ok, I have a medicine to help. It's not available in the UK, but when you get back home, maybe you can ask your own doctor for something to help you. Ok?"

I nod. I hate taking tablets, but he really isn't giving me a choice seeing as he has popped it in my mouth for me.

"Under the tongue…" he directs and I do as he says; the thing dissolves almost instantly.

"You may feel drunk. But good drunk, like happy, excitable and then you'll probably sleep."

And my god, he isn't lying. This tablet is doing serious things, and I haven't even left my seat yet.

CHAPTER THIRTY
HAPPY BIRTHDAY TO ME!

"And then Alejandro, mi oui she can bein mon adios amigo o si mi casa es su casa en le fromage."

"Sorry pal, she has been given strong medication, and she currently thinks she can speak fluent Spanish," Jay informs the confused-looking taxi driver who is taking us home.

"Ah!" I flap my hands away towards Jay as if he is speaking rubbish. "Mi fluente en Espanol. Mi like bilingual. Mi like Shakira, Shakira." I clap my hands together loudly as if a beat just dropped in my head. "OOOH I'm on tonight and my hips don't lie and I'm starting to feel this vibe, Como see llama, I'm Bonita, Chiquita, Sheniquia, Fajitas…"

I'm still carrying on as we pull up to the house, speaking a mix of Spanish, French and completely made-up words.

"Shall I repeat my number again, Alejandro?" He shakes his head, but I do it anyway. "So, it's ZE-HOE, siete, ocho, siete, einz, zwei, drei." I finish strong in German.

"So yeah, call us and we'll have drinks. Un poco beer, mi amigo."

And then I wave goodbye like the multilingual queen I really think I am, feeling completely satisfied that I just made a new friend.

Even though it's sunrise by the time we get home, the doctor definitely didn't lie about the sleep part. I am out like a light within thirty seconds of getting into bed.

When I awake, I feel much better. I feel rested but, most importantly, I feel a lot calmer than last night. And also, it's my birthday!

It's just me and Jay in the villa so nothing crazy in the way of celebrations happens. We go to the local store, and I pick up a chocolate cake for later. We then get on a train down to Almeria and spend most of the day window shopping and sitting in pretty cafés along the beach. I speak to my dad, mum and sister at various times in the day who wish me a happy birthday. Dad's phone call is a little more awkward because I need to tell him that actually, it's just me now, as the girls went home.

I can hear the disappointment in his voice, and I can tell he is pissed off that they've left me, but he shakes it off quickly and keeps the tone light.

"Ah well, Chlo, fuck 'em. When you want to come home just let me know and I'll book your ticket."

"Thanks Dad. I think I'm going to stick it out a bit longer here, just in case – there's still a chance."

"I'll keep everything crossed for you, but there's no shame in coming home you know. You tried and that's more than most people do."

When I get off the phone, I realise I do feel proud of myself – no matter what happens, nobody can say I've not been determined. And I think that is something huge to celebrate when just a couple of months ago I felt like my life was over. I couldn't even make it to my local bar with friends and yet here I am, I have been in Spain with limited money and no real clue, but I had an idea, and I had hope, and that is massively brave in itself.

And I have learned so much. I have learned I love Spain. I have learned that sometimes a change of scenery does you the world of good. I have learned that even with anxiety, I have been capable of achieving some great things, or at the very least, giving it my best efforts. I have learned that I want good things for myself. I have learned that I can be happy – it doesn't always come easily, but it is within me. Anxiety has tricked me a lot because although it has made me believe horrible things, underneath it all there is still a girl who loves to live.

CHAPTER THIRTY-ONE

LIFE

I came home. But I gave it my all and even though the dream didn't happen as I had hoped, I have no regrets.

I moved into a small flat in Tunbridge Wells with Jay who decided to leave Spain as well and come back to England with me. Although he loved the adventure, he too felt a little stuck and lonely in that rural town. It's probably the best place in the world if you're retired, but probably a little too much off the grid if you're only young.

Jay and I were in a relationship, but I haven't really gone into too much depth about that in this book. The reason for that is that there just isn't really much to say. The best thing to come out of that relationship is my beautiful baby girl, who is now a fully grown teenager who I expect will have her own bright ideas and adventures like I did one day. Jay and I weren't in love, and I think he'd agree. It was just convenient that we found each other when we did. He helped me a lot when I was in Spain and then when it was time for me to leave, I was a good excuse for him to come back to England as well.

We broke up four months after our daughter was born. And after she turned six months old, it would be almost thirteen years until we'd see or hear from him again. Jay has his own life, and he chose not to be a part of ours and that is ok. I used to fight hard for him to stay present for his daughter but sometimes you have to sit back and just let people make their own decisions, even if you think they're wrong or unfair.

Since I was eighteen years old, I have had some wonderful moments in my life. My dad bought a house in Florida and I got to fly out with my daughter when she was only two years old and spend two weeks out there. I've met great people, been to awesome places and I even eventually met the love of my life and had another baby, a little boy this time. Then in 2017, our children and a whole bunch of family and friends came out to watch us get married on Daytona Beach in Florida.

Anxiety has always been there; it's usually just lying in the background but occasionally over the years it has reared its ugly head and I have had to claw my way back again. I have come to accept that anxiety will always be a part of me, and I will no doubt spend the rest of my life battling it, but I have things in life that are worth the battle. And when things do get bad, which they have, I remind myself that I have beaten this. Time and time again. I thought my life was over at seventeen and I ended up abroad, trying to become a bloody ex-pat. After the birth of my son, I had such severe post-natal depression and anxiety that I was convinced that my life would never be the same again. And yet I ended up in Florida, married and taking my kids to the Disney Parks, having the best time of my life.

So what I have learned is that life is a series of ups and downs – the ups make it worth it and the downs make us appreciate it. If I had given up every time I thought I was going to, I'd never have experienced the beauty that the ups have given me.

I'm not cured. People online often ask me for advice and the truth is I don't have much to offer because I am still in the battle. Medication has helped me the most though and I don't think I can see myself ever coming off it to be honest. All I can say is keep talking and never be afraid to ask for help because as cliché as it sounds, you really aren't alone. Although anxiety and depression can make us feel isolated, it's surprising these days just how many people can relate.

I also really believe in the 'let them' rule now. Which basically means that we stop trying to control what other people do around us.

If they want to leave... **let them.**
If they choose someone else... **let them.**
If they don't support you... **let them.**
If they don't invite you... **let them.**

Stop wasting your energy trying to control or change other people.

Let them show who they really are. And then YOU can choose what you do next.

@*Mel* ROBBINS

I say no to things if I think it'll be bad for my mental health. And I stop beating myself up as much as I used to. I didn't make it to university, and I haven't been able to hold down jobs for too long, because of my anxiety. But it hasn't stopped me from trying. I have always given my jobs my all, I have *always* tried and that's enough.

And you know what else? Some of the best people in this world have battled some kind of mental illness and I think it makes them better people. Because you learn to appreciate so much more in life. Nobody appreciates a simple family beach day more than someone who once couldn't even leave their bedroom. So if that's you, just know that you're the best kind of person.

CHAPTER THIRTY-TWO
MUM

I feel like I need a chapter in this book to talk about my mum because I'm sure from a lot of these chapters, you probably think she sounded awful. I really wrestled with myself over just how honest I wanted to be about my mum, especially as she isn't here anymore. I worried that it would come across as disrespectful. But I also felt like I needed to tell my truth, and I think that's important when you're explaining how you ended up in a mental health unit.

Sometime after I returned from Spain, my mum actually ended up on several medications for her own mental health, but more importantly, she joined a place called The Hub, which is a mental health resource centre that completely changed her life. Suddenly, she was up and out of the house by nine o'clock in the morning so she could get to The Hub and spend her day there. The days of her sleeping in until late afternoon, usually hungover, were gone. Mum joined first as a patient but ended up staying on as a volunteer where she helped so many people. So much so that after she passed away, The Hub named a wellness café after her.

When I look back now, although a lot of it still hurts, I feel like I understand better. I'm not excusing any of the behaviour, but I realise now that she was suffering from her own illnesses. I also learned as I got older that my mum was a victim of abuse when she was a child, mostly from her mum's boyfriend but also whilst in care. I think these things that happened to my mum made it harder for her to show love and give it freely. I also think that she found it hard to trust and this meant she spent a lot of her life on the defensive and ready to attack. But The Hub helped her become a completely different version of herself.

It took some time, but I'd say from the age of twenty-three until she passed away when I was twenty-nine, I got the best version of Mum. And that's when our better times happened.

My mum was at the end of the phone whenever I needed her, even at three o'clock in the morning, and she'd never sound the slightest bit put out at being woken up. She knew if I was calling that late, it was because I was anxious. She'd answer and I'd always say, *"Mum please talk shit to me as a distraction."*

And she did. Literal random rubbish. Even down to how many letters the postman delivered to her that morning. But she'd waffle on for an hour or more if she had to, until the anxiety passed.

My mum was also, without a doubt, one of the

funniest, most quick-witted people I have ever met. Arguing with her was futile, her comeback game was too strong. She was one of only a few people on this earth who could really make me belly laugh. I'll forever miss that.

After the birth of my two children, Mum came over to my flat regularly, usually completely unannounced, two or three times a week, sometimes more. She was a very present Nana and a brilliant one. My god, I am grateful that my children got the best version of my mum because the love she was able to give was everything. Even though, at the time, I used to see her car pull up and roll my eyes and think *again?* She's here, *again!?* But I'd give anything for that now. I am grateful she kept turning up as much as she did. Maybe she was making up for lost time.

In my lifetime, I got two versions of my mum. The worst and the best. It's important to know that I forgive her for the things that happened when she was at her worst and actually, I am beyond proud of the help she got for herself. I never thought I'd see the day, but she turned everything around, which just goes to show, it's never too late.

In 1998, Mum took me to watch The Spice Girls at Wembley Stadium. I was obsessed with them when I was a child. I remember vividly that when the song "Mama" was performed, the whole stadium joined in, singing along with those wands lit up, looking like a sea of stars in the dark. My mum pulled me onto her lap and she swayed me as we both sang along. It's a memory I'll never forget because it reminds me that the love was *always* there, she just lost her way for a while.

And she'd be pleased to know I'm also now a massive ABBA fan – maybe those 3am calls singing "Fernando" rubbed off on me in the end.

I hope this chapter helps you understand a little more. Mental health comes out in so many ways, and it can change who we are and who we want to be. But I'll never not admire the strength it takes to get better.

END

COMING SOON...
F*** SAKE, MUM'S DEAD

"You can't smoke in here." The doctor panics when Mum lights up a cigarette. Something I'm sure has never happened in a doctor's surgery.

"Since when?!"

"Since 2007, when it was banned indoors."

It's 2016 now. It's only been a law for nine years.

Mum stubs her cigarette out on the side of her Silk Cut packet and drops it back in her black handbag.

"Carol, we've got the results back from your function test and we can see that at the moment, your kidneys are working at 9%, which I'm afraid to say is quite worrisome and serious, so we will need to look at treatment plans immediately."

"I don't have a clue what you just said, doctor."

"It basically means you are in stage five kidney failure."

"How many stages are there?"

"Five. So, this is what we call end stage."

"Jesus." Mum lights another cigarette. "You probably should have led with that."

"So, we'll be looking at getting you started on dialysis by next week."

"God, that sounds horrible. What if I don't want dialysis?"

"Then you'll probably die within a month or so."

Mum puffs on the cigarette. "You just really keep dishing out the good news don't you."

"If you choose not to have dialysis, we can talk you through end-of-life care options instead."

"Can't I just have like one of those pigs' kidneys or something?"

"No, it doesn't work like that. It has to be a human and it has to be a match."

"I don't know what to say. I thought it was just cystitis."

"Kidney disease doesn't always present with the most obvious symptoms, I know. I'm sorry if it's a shock. Is there anyone I can call for you?"

"One of my daughters perhaps, but I don't know. I don't want to worry them. Chloe gets anxious like me you see, she'll panic."

"I understand. Shall I send off a referral for dialysis?"

"Yes please."

"Is there anything else I can do for you before you go?"

"Can you just help me have as long as possible? I really want to see my grandchildren grow up a bit more."

Printed in Great Britain
by Amazon